EASY
ITALIAN
COOKBOOK

EASY
ITALIAN
COOKBOOK

JENNIFER DONOVAN

THE STEP-BY-STEP GUIDE TO DELICIOUSLY EASY ITALIAN FOOD AT HOME

DUNCAN BAIRD PUBLISHERS
LONDON

Easy Italian Cookbook
Jennifer Donovan

This edition first published in the United Kingdom and Ireland in 2010 by
Duncan Baird Publishers Ltd
Sixth Floor
Castle House
75–76 Wells Street
London W1T 3QH

Conceived, created and designed by Duncan Baird Publishers

Managing Editor: Grace Cheetham
Editor: Cécile Landau
Managing Designer: Manisha Patel
Designer: Luana Gobbo
Studio Photography: William Lingwood
Photography Assistant: Alice Deuchar
Stylists: Bridget Sargeson and Stella Sargeson (food)
    and Helen Trent (props)

British Library Cataloguing-in-Publication Data:
A CIP record for this book is available from the British Library

ISBN: 978-1-84483-932-2

10 9 8 7 6 5 4 3 2 1

Typeset in Spectrum and Univers
Colour reproduction by Scanhouse, Malaysia
Printed in Singapore by Imago

To my darling husband, who has always encouraged me to
pursue my dreams, and to my two sons, Chris and James,
who always tell it like it is.

Author's acknowledgments

My sincere thanks go to Grace Cheetham, my wonderful editor and
mentor, for sharing her enormous experience and talent and for having
faith in me. Thank you also to the skilled team at Duncan Baird, who put
my book together and turned it into something special. It has been a joy.

Publisher's note

While every care has been taken in compiling the recipes for this book,
Duncan Baird Publishers, or any other persons who have been involved
in working on this publication, cannot accept responsibility for any errors
or omissions, inadvertent or not, that may be found in the recipes or text,
nor for any problems that may arise as a result of preparing one of these
recipes. If you are pregnant or breastfeeding or have any special dietary
requirements or medical conditions, it is advisable to consult a medical
professional before following any of the recipes contained in this book.

Notes on the recipes

Unless otherwise stated:
• Use medium eggs
• Use fresh herbs
• Do not mix metric and imperial measurements
• 1 tsp = 5ml
  1 tbsp = 15ml
  1 cup = 250ml

CONTENTS

INTRODUCTION

It is hard to pinpoint the exact reason for the enduring popularity of Italian food. It could be the relaxed homely style of so many dishes; the wealth of delicious, fresh ingredients used or the infectious delight and regional pride that Italians take in their cuisine. But none of these factors seems to account for it entirely. Italian food simply has a heart that runs deep within.

Despite modern pressures, food remains of central importance to Italian life. Sharing the table with family and friends is preserved as a ritual to this day, with its roots firmly planted in Italian values and traditions.

In the past, it was possible to divide Italy geographically according to its culinary heritage. Linked closely to its economic background, the cuisine of Italy could be loosely divided between the affluent north and the more rural south. Fresh eggs and pasta, butter, rich risotto and creamy polenta once characterized the northern regions, while the southern parts favoured olive oil, dried pastas, pizza and tomatoes. Today, however, with increased migration around the country and the movement from rural life to city life, these culinary boundaries have blurred.

Despite this, regional boundaries remain important to the Italian people and their economy. Each region proudly produces speciality foods, including many noted cheeses and cured meats, and the provenance of each of these is strictly protected. In much the same way as France protects the provenance of its wines and other foods, Italy has developed a system known as the *denominazione d'origine protetta*, which identifies and protects the integrity and quality of a host of local products.

Italian cuisine is generally fairly simple and it is because of this simplicity that it relies heavily for its success on the best quality ingredients. Visit any town in Italy, large or small, and you will be able to find a market bursting with locally grown fruit and vegetables, where gleaming aubergines compete for attention next to dazzling red peppers and golden courgette flowers, while the heady scent of fresh basil fills the air. The colour, aroma and bustle of daily living in Italy can be intoxicating.

Italian towns and cities are bursting with tiny bars, serving espresso in the morning and something stronger as the day wears on. Family-run trattorias, always friendly and welcoming, can be found dotted around the streets of most neighbourhoods, and tables and chairs spill out from the numerous cafés that crowd around Italy's many piazzas. Food is something to be celebrated; something to be lingered over and shared. It is hard not to fall in love with Italy and its cuisine.

The *Easy Italian Cookbook* is designed to show you how simple it is to bring the true flavours of Italy into your own kitchen. It will take you through an understanding of some of the basic ingredients and equipment used and will guide you, step by step, through a wonderful selection of deliciously easy recipes.

You will find the recipes in the book arranged in the same order they would appear on a typical Italian table – antipasti, soup, pasta, gnocchi and risotto, meat and fish, vegetable dishes and salads, and finally desserts. You will also find a collection of menu plans to suit a wide range of specific occasions, which you can follow or adapt to your own needs. Soon your family and friends will be savouring the joys of Italian food.

PART 1

THE BASICS

*A set of simple "foundation" recipes and techniques lies at the **heart** of every **great** cuisine. In this section you will find all the **basics** you will need to create wonderful Italian **meals**, ranging from recipes for simple stocks and sauces and deliciously **light** fresh pasta to **traditional**-style breads.*

*Keep things **simple** by making the recipes work for you. Although the stocks take time to reduce down for **optimal** flavour, they can be made well in advance. Prepare them when you have a spare moment – they can then be left to **bubble** away **happily** for hours while you carry on with something else – and keep them in the freezer for up to three months, so that they are **ready** when you need them.*

***Fresh** bread and pizza dough can be made in advance, too, then refrigerated overnight, ready to bake the next day. Many of the **sauces** – such as pesto and the basic tomato sauce for **pasta** – can be made several days ahead and kept in an airtight jar in the fridge until needed. Others, however, such as the salsa verde and béchamel, always **taste** better when they are freshly made.*

INGREDIENTS

BALSAMIC VINEGAR

Balsamic vinegar is an aged Italian vinegar from the Modena area and dates back to the 16th century. To qualify as balsamic, it must be aged for a minimum of 12 years (and can be aged for up to 150 years!), which is why the authentic product is relatively expensive. There are many inferior products on the market labelled as "balsamic" vinegar. When buying, always look for the initials MO on the label, which indicates that it was made in Modena and that it has been aged correctly.

CHEESE

Fontina – A semi-hard cheese, it has excellent melting properties. It is made from unpasteurized cow's milk.

Gorgonzola – Made from cow's milk, this delicious blue cheese is traditionally produced in the Lombardy region. It is aged for three to six months and varies in texture from slightly creamy to extremely creamy.

Mascarpone – Produced all over Italy, mascarpone is made from coagulated double cream. It is used in both savoury and sweet dishes, but most commonly in desserts – it is the central ingredient in the ever-popular tiramisù ("pick-me-up" trifle, page 169).

Mozzarella – Most of what is termed mozzarella is made from cow's milk. But the finest mozzarella is produced from buffalo milk, mainly in the southern regions of Italy. Buffalo mozzarella has a higher percentage of fat and therefore has a much creamier taste. Also, the fresher the mozzarella, the creamier the texture, and it will taste better, too. Small bite-sized balls of buffalo mozzarella are available, which are perfect for using in salads.

Parmesan – Parmesan, or *Parmigiano Reggiano* to give it its full Italian name, is rightly one of Italy's most famous cheeses, with recorded descriptions of it dating back as early as the 11th century. Authentic *Parmigiano Reggiano* is produced by a co-operative of around 350 cheesemakers from the provinces of Parma, Reggio Emilia, Modena, Mantua and Bologna. Milk from other regions cannot be used.

Pecorino – Made from sheep's milk, this cheese is available in a number of different styles. One of the most widely used in cooking is the hard *Pecorino Romano* from the Lazio region of Italy around the city of Rome – hence the name.

Ricotta – This soft whey cheese is a by-product of making pecorino. Often used in cooking, it is also great with fresh fruit.

Taleggio – This semi-soft, creamy cheese is made from cow's milk and has a maturation period of just 10 weeks. Usually sold as squares, it is often served with fruit as a simple and delicious ending to a meal. It can also be used in cooking.

CREAM

Although it has a milk-fat content of around 48 per cent, double cream is used for the recipes in this book because it has the advantage of not separating when cooked. It can also be whipped.

EGGS

Unless otherwise specified, medium-sized eggs should be used for all the recipes in this book.

FLOUR

The best type of flour to use for making bread is commonly labelled "strong" flour. This has a higher gluten content than regular plain or all-purpose flour. Gluten is the protein found in flour that affects the texture of any baked goods made with it. Using a flour containing a high level of gluten is one of the keys to successful bread-making.

For making pasta, the best type of flour to use is very finely milled flour. It is often available as 00 flour or semolina flour. This very soft flour results in a more tender, pliable pasta.

GELATINE

Although once difficult to find in supermarkets and grocery stores, leaf gelatine is now available widely. It comes in solid sheets that need to be soaked in cold water until they soften – they will then resemble a piece of wet plastic film. Do not soak them in hot water, as they will dissolve. Once the gelatine is wet, it will dissolve instantly when stirred into a small amount of hot liquid and can then be used as directed. Leaf gelatine is generally quicker to use than powdered gelatine (see below). Four sheets will set approximately 600ml/1 pint/2½ cups of liquid.

Where required, powdered gelatine can be used instead of leaf gelatine for the recipes in this book – 10g/¼oz will set around 500ml/18fl oz/2 cups of liquid. To use, put 50ml/2fl oz/⅓ cup of cold water in a bowl and sprinkle over the 10g/¼oz of powdered gelatine. Leave it to stand for five minutes, then place the bowl over a pan of gently simmering water – so that the base does not touch the water – until the gelatine mixture becomes clear. Use as directed in the recipe.

HERBS AND SPICES

Basil – This deliciously pungent herb is one of the most widely used in Italian cooking.

Bay leaf – Available dried or fresh, bay leaves are often used in stocks and soups to impart a subtle but distinctive flavour.

Black pepper – A staple in the Italian kitchen, it is at its best and most pungent when used freshly ground.

Chillies – Italian cooking most commonly uses red chillies, either fresh or dried. Bear in mind that the smaller the chilli, the hotter it generally is.

Nutmeg – The seed of a plant native to Indonesia, this small nut-shaped spice can be purchased whole or ground. The best flavour comes from using the whole spice, freshly grated. It gives a warm, slightly spicy lift to recipes.

Oregano – This small, soft-leaved herb is usually added to soups and casseroles at the very last minute, giving them a wonderfully fresh flavour.

Parsley – Although available dried, fresh parsley is better by far. The flat-leaf variety is most commonly used in Italy.

Rosemary – Usually just the leaves of this herb, stripped from the stems and chopped, are used. Rosemary stems are tough, although some recipes call for whole stalks, which cook in a soup or stew and are then removed before serving.

Saffron – Derived from the crocus plant, only small quantities of this highly aromatic spice are needed. It also imparts a yellow colour to dishes. The best comes from Spain.

Sage – This herb has a distinctive long, fleshy leaf and a really pungent flavour. It can be used to add a wonderful richness and depth to many recipes.

Thyme – A very common addition to Italian dishes, thyme is used to flavour soups, stews and traditional bean recipes.

MARSALA WINE

Made from a blend of boiled grape juice, white wine and distilled alcohol, this sweet fortified wine was traditionally made in the west of Sicily. It is said to have been originally produced by an Englishman, John Woodhouse, in the late 18th century, as an alternative to sherry.

MUSHROOMS

Italy has over 60 different varieties of mushrooms available and a visit to any local market in the autumn will reward you with a spectacular display. Porcini are one of the most popular mushrooms in Italy, but numerous other varieties are also used. The flavour of mushrooms intensifies when they are dried and you will often see sliced porcini sold this way. In order to use them, they need to be soaked for at least 30 minutes in hot water. The soaking liquid will also impart a wonderful flavour to many dishes, such as risotto, but needs to be strained carefully before use to remove any grit.

NUTS

Almonds – These are used liberally throughout Italy, especially in Sicily, where they grow in abundance.

Hazelnuts – Often used in sweet dishes, hazelnuts can be eaten raw but develop a fuller flavour when toasted. For most dishes, it is best to remove as much of the papery outer skin as possible by rubbing the toasted nuts against a sieve.

Pine nuts – Pine nuts are the small edible seeds that grow in the cone of some species of pine tree. They are a very popular addition to many Italian dishes. Although delicious when eaten raw, their flavouring is enhanced considerably by toasting. Take care, however, when doing this, as they are high in fat and will burn very easily.

Walnuts – Another popular choice of nut throughout Italy, walnuts are a central ingredient in panforte. Like most nuts, they can become bitter quite quickly – if shelled, they should ideally be stored in the fridge, where they will keep well for up to six months. They can also be frozen for up to 12 months.

OLIVES AND OLIVE OIL

Italian cooks use a very wide range of different green and black olives in their dishes. The colour of an olive is generally of no importance, but the flavour will vary greatly, depending on the variety, the region of origin and method that has been used for curing.

Extra-virgin olive oil is made from the first pressing of the olives and is therefore considered to be of the very best quality. It should have low acidity with a distinctive fruity aroma and flavour. Which particular variety of extra-virgin olive oil you choose to use is a matter of personal taste. Differences in flavour can be quite marked and will depend on the variety of olives used, their growing conditions and the way in which they were harvested and bottled. Heating olive oil to a high temperature generally causes its flavour to suffer, so extra-virgin olive oil is not recommended for cooking, but is usually reserved for drizzling over food and for preparing salad dressings.

Other types of olive oils are chemically processed after the first pressing and many of them are blended with other oils before bottling.

All olive oil should be stored in a dark, airtight container, away from extremes of temperature and bright light. It should not be kept for more than two years.

PARMA HAM AND PANCETTA

Parma ham (*prosciutto di Parma*) and pancetta are just two of the cured meats for which Italy is deservedly famous. Parma ham is one of the most celebrated products of the region of Emilia-Romagna, which is renowned for its superb cuisine and wide range of gastronomic specialities. Parmesan cheese is another noted product of the region and the pigs there are fed on by-products from the making of this cheese, which is what gives Parma ham its distinctive flavour. Parma ham is most commonly served, sliced very thinly, as part of an antipasto platter. Many other varieties of prosciutto are also available throughout Italy.

Pancetta is made from cured belly pork and is also produced all over Italy. Being relatively high in fat, it is rarely cooked and eaten on its own, but is often chopped up and added to soups and casseroles, adding a deliciously rich flavour.

PASSATA

This is strained, crushed tomato pulp that is useful for adding to soups, pasta sauces and other savoury recipes. It can be chunky or smooth and is now widely available, ready-made in cartons and jars, from most supermarkets. It can also be made very easily at home from fresh, ripe tomatoes by simply skinning them, then pressing them through a sieve to remove the seeds.

PASTA

Two broad categories of pasta are used in Italy – fresh and dried – and, as most Italian cooks will tell you, fresh is not necessarily the best, both having their own place in the cuisine. The use of fresh homemade pasta is generally confined to the flat noodle and sheet varieties, which include pappardelle, tagliatelle and lasagne, as well as the stuffed pastas, such as ravioli and tortellini.

Dried pasta, often made from semolina, is used for the more solid shapes, such as spaghetti, rigatoni and penne.

Most Italian cooks today use eggs and flour to prepare homemade pasta, although in the past, in poorer parts of Italy, it was usually made with just flour and water. Because it is more porous than semolina pasta, it tends to be more absorbent and is therefore best served with creamy, buttery sauces. By comparison, dried pasta is good with oil-based and more substantial sauces – particularly the shaped pastas, as they "catch" such rich sauces well.

POLENTA

Made from coarsely ground cornmeal, polenta is an Italian staple, particularly in the northern regions. There are two varieties – the traditional slow-cooking type and the instant variety (see page 27). Although both are widely used throughout Italy, most traditional cooks would choose the slow-cooking variety for its superior flavour and texture.

PULSES

Pulses, such as lentils, borlotti beans and cannellini beans, are popular in Italy. Although available tinned, dried pulses can be kept indefinitely, so are a useful store-cupboard standby. The beans are generally soaked overnight to tenderize them, then rinsed and boiled for up to an hour, until they are tender.

RISOTTO RICE

Several different types of rice can be used to make risotto, but the three most popular varieties are Arborio, Vialone Nano and Carnaroli. Arborio produces a "stickier" result and makes an excellent choice for really hearty risotto dishes, although it needs greater care in cooking to prevent it from becoming too stodgy. Vialone has a slightly looser consistency and gives a little more resistance to the bite. It is popular for making seafood risottos. Carnaroli, developed in the 1940s, is a relative newcomer. It is considered by many Italian cooks to be superior to all other varieties of risotto rice, as it results in dishes with a well-balanced, firm yet creamy consistency.

VEGETABLES AND FRUIT

All over Italy, market stalls and greengrocers' shelves are brimming with really fresh, top quality fruit and vegetables, which are central to the success of so many Italian dishes. It is best to always try to buy what is currently in season and in approximately the quantity you need at the time, as the flavour of such produce, however well kept, will deteriorate over time. Most of the fruit and vegetables used in this book, including asparagus, aubergines, courgettes, fennel, peppers, tomatoes, rocket, lemons, strawberries and peaches, are readily available, even if only for a short season every year. Cavolo nero is one of the few exceptions and may be harder to find. This dark green, long-leafed cabbage from the Tuscan region can, however, be substituted with any other variety of cabbage, if unavailable.

YEAST

Three different types of yeast can be used for baking. The first is fresh yeast, which is often only available from a local baker or small specialist shop, such as an organic wholefood outlet or a delicatessen. It comes as a compressed solid and must be stored in the fridge. The other two types are both forms of dried yeast, sold as granules in packets and readily available from the local supermarket. One, simply labelled as dried yeast, will need to be activated in warm water before use, while the other, labelled as easy-blend yeast, can simply be stirred in with the other dry ingredients, such as flour.

Many cooks now prefer to use some form of dried yeast – especially the easy-blend variety – as it can be stored in the cupboard for a very long time, tends to be reliable and is extremely quick and easy to use. Also, the difference between the flavour of bread that has been made with fresh yeast and that made with dried yeast is very difficult indeed to discern. All the recipes in this book involving yeast give instructions for using the easy-blend variety, but either of the other two types may be substituted if you wish.

If you prefer to use fresh yeast, or it is the only type you have available, it is important to activate it before mixing it in with the other ingredients. This is done by warming about 125ml/4fl oz/½ cup of liquid (milk or water depending on the recipe) and pouring it into a mug or small bowl, then adding ½ teaspoon of sugar, stirring well and crumbling the fresh yeast over the top. Stir gently to just combine, then leave the mixture in a warm place until it starts to foam. This should take around 10 minutes. The yeast is now ready to use.

Basic dried yeast must also be blended with a little warm water to activate it. Make sure that the liquid is not too hot – this will kill the yeast and make it inactive and you will end up with a "rock" instead of a well-risen loaf of bread. Once the yeast has begun to foam, add it to the flour mixture with the remaining ingredients, according to the recipe instructions.

Always remember that dried yeast has twice the potency of fresh yeast. For every 15g/½oz of fresh yeast, you will need to use only 7g/¼oz of dried yeast.

EQUIPMENT

CAST-IRON GRIDDLE PAN

This heavy pan has raised ridges across its inside base that leave an attractive pattern on food cooked in it. The food will also acquire a wonderful chargrilled flavour. Cast-iron griddle pans can be used to cook all types of meat, fish and vegetables quickly and easily, often without the need for any added fat, and so offer the bonus of a really healthy way of cooking.

CHEESE GRATER

There are a variety of designs on the market to choose from. Small micro-plane graters are particularly good for very hard cheeses, such as Parmesan.

CHOPPING BOARD

A good collection of chopping boards is essential. Make sure that they are non-porous and therefore can be cleaned well.

COLANDER

A big colander is helpful for draining large quantities of pasta.

ELECTRIC MIXER

Both the hand-held and free-standing varieties are very useful in the kitchen, especially for keen bakers.

FOOD PROCESSOR

These machines are far from essential, but very convenient for quickly making up pastry and pasta and bread dough.

GARLIC CRUSHER

Garlic can be crushed on a board with the side of a cook's knife (sprinkle the garlic with salt to help with the crushing action), but many cooks find it quicker to use a garlic crusher.

ICE CREAM MACHINE

If you truly love gelato, then this can be a good investment. A wide variety is available, from battery-operated models to large machines with their own built-in freezer.

IMMERSION BLENDER

Sometimes known as a "wand", this type of electric blender can process food without having to remove it from the pan it has been cooked in. It is great for puréeing soups and sauces.

JUICE EXTRACTOR

These range from simple hand-operated citrus presses to large electrical appliances that can extract the juice from any type of fruit or vegetable.

KNIVES

The cook's most important tool, when preparing any type of cuisine, is a set of sharp, good quality knives. This should include a 20cm/8in all-purpose cook's knife, one or two small paring knives and a serrated-edged knife. Other knives, such as a carving or boning knife, can be added to the basic kit as required. For preparing herbs, Italian cooks often prefer to use a *mezzaluna*, which consists of a curved-blade knife with a handle at each end that is used in a rocking motion to chop herbs really finely.

PASTA MACHINE

Many Italians still roll out pasta by hand, but a pasta machine makes the job much easier. It is best to buy the type that clamps onto a worktop and pushes the pasta out through a set of rollers that is rotated by hand. Electric machines that also mix the pasta dough tend to give a poorer result.

POTATO RICER

Cooked potatoes are pressed through this device, resembling a large garlic crusher, to create a soft purée – great for gnocchi.

SAUCEPANS

You will need a full range of saucepans, from the very small (for melting butter or heating milk) to the very large (for boiling water for pasta or for preparing stocks and stews). Remember that pans with a thick, heavy base will conduct heat better, and so cook more quickly and evenly, than cheaper, more lightweight pans.

SAUTÉ PAN

This is an invaluable tool in any kitchen. A sauté pan differs from a frying pan in that it has slightly higher, sloping edges, making it perfect for pan-frying meats and making sauces. The pan's wide surface will allow excess liquid to evaporate easily where necessary and the sloping edges will allow the steam to escape rather than staying in the pan and steaming the food. A handy size for a sauté pan is approximately 25cm/10in in diameter.

SLOTTED SPOON

This simple utensil will prove endlessly useful for lifting cooked food out of hot water or fat, without having to drain the entire pan.

SPRINGFORM CAKE TINS

The springform design of the cake tin makes removing the contents much easier. They are available in a variety of sizes.

TONGS

Tongs make turning over food, such as a piece of meat or fish, halfway through cooking, really quick and easy.

VEGETABLE PEELER

This is useful, not only for removing the skin from potatoes and carrots, but also for slicing them up really thinly. The long type with a pointed tip can also be used to core apples.

WOODEN SPOONS

Cheap and hard-wearing, a set of these is always handy, as they can be used for stirring or mixing any food, hot or cold.

STOCKS AND SAUCES

BEEF STOCK
BRODO DI MANZO

MAKES 2 LITRES/3½ PINTS/8 CUPS
PREPARATION TIME: 35 MINUTES   COOKING TIME: 4 HOURS

1kg/2lb 4oz **beef** bones

1 **onion** (skin left on), roughly chopped

1 **carrot**, roughly chopped

1 stick **celery**, roughly chopped

4 **black peppercorns**

1 **bay leaf**

1 sprig **thyme**

1 small handful **flat-leaf parsley**, roughly chopped

4 litres/7 pints/16 cups cold **water**

1 **PREHEAT** the oven to 200°C/400°F/Gas 6. Place the beef bones on a baking tray and roast in the hot oven for around 30 minutes or until well browned all over.

2 **REMOVE** any fat from the bones, then transfer them to a large saucepan. Add all of the remaining ingredients.

3 **BRING** to the boil. Skim off any froth and sediment from the surface, then lower the heat and leave to simmer very gently for 4 hours, skimming often. Remove from the heat and leave to cool, then strain.

4 **REFRIGERATE** overnight, then remove any fat that has collected on the surface. Use as required. It will keep for 3–4 days in the fridge and up to 3 months in the freezer.

CHICKEN STOCK
BRODO DI POLLO

MAKES 2 LITRES/3½ PINTS/8 CUPS
PREPARATION TIME: 15 MINUTES   COOKING TIME: 2½ HOURS

If you have trouble finding chicken carcasses, substitute with chicken wings. They will render more fat, but this can easily be removed from the surface of the stock after it has been chilled overnight in the fridge.

1kg/2lb 4oz fresh **chicken** carcasses, chopped

1 **onion** (skin left on), cut into quarters

1 **carrot**, roughly chopped

1 bulb **garlic**, cut in half horizontally

1 stick **celery**, roughly chopped

4 **black peppercorns**

1 small handful **flat-leaf parsley**, roughly chopped

2 **bay leaves**

6 litres/10½ pints/24 cups cold **water**

1 **PLACE** all of the ingredients in a large saucepan and bring gently to the boil.

2 **SKIM** off any foam and sediment from the surface, then lower the heat and leave to simmer for around 2½ hours.

3 **STRAIN** the stock through a fine sieve into a clean bowl. Cover and leave to cool completely.

4 **REFRIGERATE** overnight, then skim off any fat from the surface and use as required. It will keep for 3–4 days in the fridge and up to 3 months in the freezer.

FISH STOCK
BRODO DI PESCE

MAKES 2 LITRES/3½ PINTS/8 CUPS
PREPARATION TIME: 10 MINUTES   COOKING TIME: 20 MINUTES

15g/½oz **butter**

1 **onion**, roughly chopped

1kg/2lb 4oz **fish** bones, washed and chopped

125ml/4fl oz/½ cup **dry white wine**

2.5 litres/4½ pints/10 cups cold **water**

1 **bay leaf**

4 **black peppercorns**

1 small handful **flat-leaf parsley**, roughly chopped

1 small stick **celery**, roughly chopped

1 MELT the butter in a large saucepan over a low heat. Add the onion and cook for 2–3 minutes, until soft but not brown. Add the fish bones and cook for about 1 minute, then pour over the white wine, turn up the heat, and boil until all the wine has evaporated.

2 ADD the water, bay leaf, peppercorns, parsley and celery and bring to the boil. Skim off any froth and sediment from the surface, then turn down the heat and leave to simmer gently for 20 minutes, skimming often.

3 STRAIN and leave to cool. Use as needed. It will keep for 3–4 days in the fridge and up to 3 months in the freezer.

VEGETABLE STOCK
BRODO DI VERDURA

MAKES 1.2 LITRES/2 PINTS/4¾ CUPS
PREPARATION TIME: 15 MINUTES   COOKING TIME: 1 HOUR

1 stick **celery**, roughly chopped, plus any leaves from the top of the stalk

1 **carrot**, roughly chopped

1 **onion**, skin removed and sliced

1 bulb **garlic**, cut in half horizontally

2 **bay leaves**

6 **black peppercorns**

1 small handful **flat-leaf parsley**, roughly chopped

1.75 litres/3 pints/7 cups cold **water**

1 PLACE all of the ingredients in a large saucepan and bring to the boil over a medium heat.

2 LOWER the heat and leave to simmer gently for 1 hour. Remove from the heat and leave to cool.

3 STRAIN the stock, pushing down on the vegetables gently to extract the maximum amount of flavour. Use as required. It will keep for up to 4 days in the fridge and for up to 3 months in the freezer.

BÉCHAMEL SAUCE

MAKES 1 LITRE/1¾ PINTS/4 CUPS
PREPARATION TIME: 10 MINUTES   COOKING TIME: 10 MINUTES

This simple white sauce makes its appearance in the lasagne recipe on page 85, but is also added to all kinds of other dishes.

1 litre/1¾ pints/4 cups **milk**

½ small **onion**

1 **bay leaf**

1 whole **clove**

85g/3oz **butter**

85g/3oz **plain flour**

salt and freshly ground **black pepper**

grating of fresh **nutmeg**

1 PLACE the milk, onion, bay leaf and clove in a medium saucepan and heat gently. As soon as the milk starts to simmer, remove from the heat and leave on one side for at least 10 minutes. Strain, discarding the solids, and set aside.

2 MELT the butter in a clean saucepan. Stir in the flour, then allow to cook over a low heat for 2–3 minutes, taking care not to let the mixture brown. Remove from the heat.

3 WHISK the milk into the butter and flour mixture, then return to a low heat and continue to whisk until the sauce is smooth and thick. Leave to simmer very gently for about 3 minutes. Season to taste with salt, pepper and nutmeg and use as required.

BLACK OLIVE TAPENADE
PASTA D'OLIVE

MAKES 250ML/9FL OZ/1 CUP
PREPARATION TIME: 15 MINUTES

200g/7oz good quality **black olives**, pitted

50g/1¾oz tinned **anchovy** fillets, rinsed

2 heaped tsp **capers**, drained and rinsed

2 cloves **garlic**, peeled

grated rind and juice of 1 **lemon**

10 tbsp **extra-virgin olive oil**

1 PLACE all of the ingredients in a blender or food processor and process until smooth.

2 STORE in the refrigerator for up to 1 month and use as required – as a flavouring or as a savoury dip with chunks of crusty fresh bread.

FRESH TOMATO SAUCE
SALSA FRESCA DI POMODORO

MAKES 500ML/17FL OZ/2 CUPS
PREPARATION TIME: 15 MINUTES   COOKING TIME: 30 MINUTES

Try to use ripe, in-season tomatoes for this recipe. Tinned tomatoes, however, can be substituted when good fresh ones are unavailable.

2 tbsp **olive oil**

1 **onion**, diced

1 clove **garlic**, crushed

1kg/2lb 4oz fresh **plum tomatoes**, peeled, deseeded and chopped

6 fresh **basil leaves**

1 tsp **balsamic vinegar**

1 tsp **sugar**

salt and freshly ground **black pepper**

1 HEAT the oil in a wide-based pan. Add the onion and cook for 3–4 minutes until it is soft and transparent. Add the garlic and cook for another minute.

2 STIR in the tomatoes, basil, balsamic vinegar and sugar and leave to simmer for 30 minutes, stirring occasionally.

3 SEASON to taste with salt and pepper, then tip into a blender or food processor and process until smooth. Use as required. It can be stored in the fridge for 2–3 days, but is best stored frozen – use within 3 months.

VARIATIONS

TOMATO AND ROASTED RED PEPPER SAUCE – Cut 2 red peppers in half lengthways, remove and discard the seeds and arrange, skin side up, on a lightly oiled baking tray. Place under a hot grill for 5–10 minutes, until the skin is really black and burnt and the flesh is just starting to soften. Remove from the grill, cover loosely with a clean cloth and set on one side until cold, then peel off the charred skin. Roughly chop the softened flesh and add to the sauce mixture along with the seasoning, at the beginning of Step 3 of the basic recipe.

TOMATO, ANCHOVY AND OLIVE SAUCE – As soon as the onions are soft and transparent (in Step 1 of the basic recipe) add 6 anchovy fillets, that have been drained and rinsed, to the pan. Cook over a low heat until the anchovies start to break up, then toss in the garlic and continue as for the basic recipe, substituting a large handful of roughly chopped flat-leaf parsley for the basil. Rinse, stone and chop a handful of green olives and stir into the smooth sauce after it has been processed in the blender or food processor.

BASIC TOMATO SAUCE FOR PIZZA

SALSA DI POMODORO PER PIZZA

MAKES 250ML/9FL OZ/1 CUP
PREPARATION TIME: 5 MINUTES   COOKING TIME: 15–20 MINUTES

This makes a thick, rich tomato sauce that is just perfect for pizza.

1 x 400g/14oz tin **tomatoes**, chopped

1 tbsp **olive oil**

1 tsp dried **basil**

1 tsp dried **oregano**

1 clove **garlic**, crushed

2 tbsp **tomato purée**

salt and freshly ground **black pepper**

1 PLACE all the ingredients in a medium-sized saucepan, seasoning to taste with salt and pepper. Bring to the boil.

2 LOWER the heat and leave to simmer for 15–20 minutes or until the sauce has thickened, stirring occasionally. Set aside to cool slightly, then transfer to a blender or food processor and process until smooth.

3 ALLOW the sauce to cool completely, then use as required. It can be stored in the fridge for up to 1 week and in the freezer for up to 3 months.

BASIL PESTO

PESTO

MAKES 250ML/9FL OZ/1 CUP
PREPARATION TIME: 15 MINUTES

This simple sauce is absolutely bursting with flavour. It can be made in advance and kept in the fridge, ready to simply stir into a plate of freshly cooked pasta to create a quick and delicious meal. To store, place in an airtight container, top with a splash of extra-virgin olive oil and refrigerate. It will keep for approximately 2 weeks.

3 large handfuls fresh **basil leaves**

25g/1oz **pine nuts**

2 large cloves **garlic**, chopped

1 tbsp **sea salt**

freshly ground **black pepper**

10 tbsp **extra-virgin olive oil**

50g/2oz **Parmesan cheese**, grated

1 PLACE the basil, pine nuts, garlic, and salt and pepper to taste in a large bowl.

2 ADD the olive oil and blend, using a hand-held mixer or blender, to form a paste. Alternatively, process the ingredients in a blender or food processor.

3 STIR in the Parmesan cheese, taste and readjust the seasoning if necessary. Use as required.

BASIC RECIPES

FRESH PASTA

SERVES 4 AS A MAIN COURSE; 8 AS A STARTER
PREPARATION TIME: 30 MINUTES
COOKING TIME: 4 MINUTES, PLUS 30 MINUTES RESTING TIME

The silky texture of freshly made pasta is well worth the effort that goes into preparing it yourself at home. For the best result, use specialized 00 flour – often labelled as "pasta flour" – which is now readily available from many supermarkets as well as speciality stores. A food processor makes mixing the dough easier, but it can also be mixed by hand. To roll out the pasta, you ideally need a good quality, manual pasta machine.

250g/9oz 00 (pasta) flour

6 large egg yolks

1 egg

1½ tbsp olive oil

1 tbsp milk

1 PLACE the flour in the bowl of a food processor. Whisk together the egg yolks, whole egg, olive oil and milk in a jug.

2 WITH the motor running, slowly pour the liquid mixture through the feeding tube onto the flour in the processor, until a soft ball of dough is just starting to form. Take care not to add too much liquid – depending on the weather, the dough may need more or less to come together. Wrap in clear film, set aside and allow to rest for 30 minutes.

3 DIVIDE the dough in two and set one half aside in a cool place, wrapped in clear film to prevent it from drying out.

4 SET the pasta machine to its widest setting and use to roll out the unwrapped half of dough. Fold the rolled dough in half and roll it once more through the machine. Repeat this process 10 more times, folding the dough in half each time before passing it through the machine.

5 CONTINUE rolling the dough in this way, but without folding it in half, and lower the setting on the machine by one notch each time, until it has passed through on the second narrowest setting (any narrower and it tends to fall apart).

6 LAY the sheet of dough on a lightly floured board. Cut into the desired shapes with a sharp knife or cutter and leave to dry.

7 REPEAT with the remaining half of the dough.

8 BRING a large pot of salted water to the boil. Add the pasta and stir well to prevent it sticking. Return to the boil, lower the heat and leave to simmer for about 4 minutes, or until the pasta has floated to the top and is paler in colour. Drain and serve immediately with your chosen sauce.

VARIATIONS

PASTA WITH FRESH HERBS – Add 3 tablespoons of finely chopped, fresh, mixed herbs – such as oregano, flat-leaf parsley and thyme – to the flour. Proceed as for basic recipe.

TOMATO PASTA – Beat 2 tablespoons of tomato purée into the egg mixture. Proceed as for the basic recipe.

SPINACH PASTA – Use only 3 egg yolks. Add 150g/5½oz cooked spinach, that has been squeezed until very dry, to flour in the food processor and pulse briefly to combine. Proceed as for the basic recipe.

"WET" POLENTA

SERVES 4   PREPARATION TIME: 10 MINUTES   COOKING TIME: 1 HOUR

With casseroles and similar dishes, polenta is usually served "wet" (sometimes described as "soft"). This means that it has simply been cooked in water or stock and served straight from the pot, so that it resembles mashed potato.

Traditional slow-cook polenta will take around 1 hour to prepare, simmering gently on the stove. You can vary the flavour by adding fresh herbs or freshly grated Parmesan cheese to it before serving. An instant variety of polenta is also available which takes very little time to prepare, although most Italians would argue that the flavour is very poor. However, for the time-starved cook it makes a good substitute.

1.4 litres/2½ pints/5½ cups **chicken stock** or **water**

175g/6oz **polenta** (not instant)

25g/1oz **butter**, cut into pieces

salt and freshly ground **black pepper**

1 BRING the water or stock to the boil in a large saucepan. Remove from the heat and whisk in the polenta in a steady stream. Lower the heat to a simmer and return to the stove.

2 SIMMER very gently for 50–60 minutes, stirring from time to time, until thick and creamy. Stir in the butter, then season to taste with salt and pepper. Keep warm until required.

"DRY" POLENTA

SERVES 4   PREPARATION TIME: 13 MINUTES
COOKING TIME: 1 HOUR 5 MINUTES, PLUS COOLING TIME

Crisp, freshly fried pieces of "dry" polenta are also very popular, served as an accompaniment to grilled meat or fish, or as a base for antipasti.

ingredients as for **"wet" polenta**

olive oil

1 PREPARE the "wet" polenta according to the instructions, left.

2 POUR the cooked "wet" polenta into a large, lightly greased baking tray and spread out to form a layer about 1cm/½in thick. Set aside and leave to cool completely.

3 CUT the cooled polenta into wedges or squares and drizzle each with a little olive oil.

4 HEAT a griddle pan or heavy-based frying pan until hot. Place the pieces of polenta in the pan and chargrill for about 2–3 minutes on each side until lightly golden. Alternatively, the polenta may be cooked under a hot grill. Use as required.

BASIC PIZZA DOUGH
PASTA BASE PER PIZZA

MAKES 2 x 30CM/12IN PIZZA BASES OR APPROXIMATELY
36 INDIVIDUAL PIZZAS
PREPARATION TIME: 25 MINUTES, PLUS 1 HOUR PROVING TIME

500g/1lb 2oz **strong white flour**, plus extra
for kneading
1 tbsp **salt**
1 tsp **sugar**
2 tsp **easy-blend yeast** *(see page 15)*
freshly ground **black pepper**
2 tbsp **olive oil**, plus extra for oiling
about 350ml/12fl oz/1½ cups warm **water**

1 MIX together the flour, salt, sugar, yeast and pepper to taste
in a large bowl and make a well in the centre.
2 POUR the olive oil into the well, then mix in with just
enough warm water to form a soft dough.
3 REMOVE the dough from the bowl and place on a lightly
floured surface. Knead for around 10 minutes, until the
dough is smooth and elastic, adding extra flour to the
surface as required.
4 PLACE the dough in a lightly oiled bowl, cover with clear
film and leave to prove in a warm place for about 1 hour,
until doubled in size.

PIZZA

MAKES 2 x 30CM/12IN PIZZAS
PREPARATION TIME: 10 MINUTES COOKING TIME: 10–15 MINUTES

1 recipe quantity **basic pizza dough** *(see left)*
1 recipe quantity **basic tomato sauce for
pizza** *(see page 24)*
topping *(see below)*

1 PREHEAT the oven to 220°C/425°F/Gas 7. Knead the risen
pizza dough on a lightly floured surface for 2–3 minutes.
2 DIVIDE the dough in half and roll out each half to fit into a
lightly greased pizza pan, about 30cm/12in in diameter.
3 SPOON over some of the tomato sauce, then add your
chosen topping. Bake in the preheated oven for about 10–15
minutes, until the topping is melted and golden. Serve.

TOPPING SUGGESTIONS
PIZZA MARGHERITA – Scatter 150g/5½oz grated mozzarella
cheese and 8 roughly torn fresh basil leaves over the tomato
sauce on the pizza base.

PIZZA AI FUNGHI – Sauté 350g/12oz sliced mushrooms in a
little olive oil until soft. Spoon over the tomato sauce on the
pizza base, then sprinkle over 55g/2oz grated mozzarella.

PIZZA MARINARA – Scatter 3 chopped garlic cloves and a
handful of chopped fresh oregano over the tomato sauce on
the pizza base. Arrange 6 anchovy fillets with 8 roughly torn
fresh basil leaves on top, then drizzle over a little olive oil.

FOCACCIA

SERVES 4–6
PREPARATION TIME: 20 MINUTES
COOKING TIME: 20 MINUTES, PLUS 1 HOUR PROVING TIME

500g/1lb 2oz **strong white flour**, plus extra
   for kneading

2 tsp **sea salt**, plus 1 tbsp, for sprinkling

½ tsp **sugar**

2 tsp **easy-blend yeast** (*see page 15*)

2 tbsp **olive oil**, plus extra for drizzling

about 325ml/11fl oz/1⅓ cups warm **water**

1 PREHEAT the oven to 230°C/450°F/Gas 8.

2 MIX the flour, sea salt, sugar and yeast together in a large
bowl and make a well in the centre.

3 POUR the olive oil into the well and mix into the flour
mixture with enough warm water to form a soft dough.

4 TIP the dough onto a lightly floured surface and knead for
about 10 minutes, or until it springs back when pressed
gently. Add extra flour to the work surface as required.

5 PLACE the dough in a clean bowl, cover with clear film
and leave in a warm place for 1 hour, until doubled in size.

6 REMOVE the dough from the bowl, place on a lightly
floured surface and knead again for 2–3 minutes until
smooth. Place on a large baking sheet and gently pull and
stretch the dough to cover the tray. Drizzle over a little
olive oil and sprinkle with the sea salt. Leave in a warm

place for 30 minutes to rise. Once the dough has risen, make
several rows of indentations across the surface.

7 BAKE in the preheated oven for 20–25 minutes, until
golden brown and slightly risen. Test to see if fully cooked
by tapping the base – it should sound hollow.

8 DRIZZLE a little more olive oil over the top and leave
to cool on a wire rack for about 15 minutes. Serve, cut
into slices.

VARIATIONS

FOCACCIA AL ROSMARINO – Mix 1 tablespoon of dried
rosemary and 1 tablespoon of finely chopped, fresh rosemary,
into the flour, salt, sugar and yeast mixture before mixing in
the olive oil and warm water to form the dough. Also, place
small sprigs of fresh rosemary in the indentations made
across the surface of the dough (see Step 6, above) just before
it goes into the oven.

FOCACCIA WITH SUN-DRIED TOMATOES – Mix
3 tablespoons of finely chopped sun-dried tomatoes into
the flour, salt, sugar and yeast mixture before mixing in the
olive oil and warm water to form the dough. Also, place
small pieces of sun-dried tomatoes in the indentations across
the surface of the dough (see Step 6, above) just before it goes
into the oven.

EVERYDAY WHITE LOAF
PANE BIANCO

MAKES 1 LARGE LOAF
PREPARATION TIME: 30 MINUTES
COOKING TIME: 40–50 MINUTES, PLUS 1 HOUR PROVING TIME

The smell of freshly baked bread is absolutely irresistible.

700g/1lb 9oz **strong white flour**, plus extra for kneading

2 tsp **easy-blend yeast** *(see page 15)*

1 tsp **sugar**

1 tbsp **salt**

250ml/9fl oz/1 cup warm **water**

250ml/9fl oz/1 cup warm **milk**

2 tbsp **extra-virgin olive oil**

olive oil, plus extra for greasing

1 **egg**, lightly beaten

2 tbsp **sesame seeds**

1 COMBINE the flour, yeast, sugar and salt in a large bowl. Make a well in the centre and set aside.

2 MIX together the warm water, warm milk and olive oil in a small bowl. Pour about three-quarters of the liquid into the well in the flour mixture and gradually mix in to form a soft dough. Use more of the remaining liquid if necessary.

3 PLACE the dough on a lightly floured surface and knead for about 10 minutes, until it springs back easily when pressed gently.

4 TRANSFER the dough to a clean, lightly oiled, large bowl. Cover with clear film and leave in a warm place for about 1 hour or until the dough has doubled in size.

5 PREHEAT the oven to 200°C/400°F/Gas 6. Place the dough on a lightly floured surface and flatten and shape it to form a large, 2.5cm/1in thick round. Brush with a little of the lightly beaten egg and roll up, tucking in the sides, to form a neat parcel.

6 GREASE an oven tray with a little more olive oil and place the shaped dough on top. Brush with the remaining beaten egg and sprinkle over the sesame seeds. Slash the top with a sharp knife in two or three places. Set aside in a warm place for a further 30 minutes until well risen.

7 SPRINKLE over a little cold water, then bake in the preheated oven for 40–50 minutes, until golden brown and well risen. To test if fully cooked, tap the base of the loaf – it should sound hollow. Leave to cool on a wire rack for at least 30 minutes before serving.

LITTLE BREADSTICKS

GRISSINI

MAKES 30 GRISSINI
PREPARATION TIME: 20 MINUTES
COOKING TIME: 18–20 MINUTES, PLUS 1 HOUR PROVING TIME

These delicious little breadsticks make a wonderful addition to a platter of antipasto. Their flavour can be varied by mixing in a small handful of finely chopped fresh herbs, such as oregano, thyme or rosemary, when preparing the dough. They can also be flavoured by sprinkling some sesame or poppy seeds, along with the crushed sea salt, over the top of the rolled-out "sausages" of dough, just before baking.

400g/14oz **strong white flour**, plus extra for kneading

2 tsp **easy-blend yeast** *(see page 15)*

1 tbsp **salt**

250ml/9fl oz/1 cup warm **water**

3 tbsp **olive oil**

2 tbsp **sea salt**, lightly crushed

1 PLACE the flour, yeast and salt into a large bowl and combine together thoroughly. Make a well in the centre and set on one side.

2 MIX together the warm water and 1 tablespoon of the olive oil in a small bowl and pour half of this into the well in the centre of the flour mixture. Gradually stir in and bring together to make a soft dough, adding more of the remaining liquid if required. The dough should be slightly sticky but not wet. Turn out onto a lightly floured surface.

3 KNEAD for about 10 minutes, until smooth and elastic. The dough should spring back when pressed gently. Transfer to a clean, lightly oiled bowl and cover with clear film. Leave in a warm place for about 1 hour until the dough has doubled in size.

4 PREHEAT the oven to 400°F/200°C/Gas 6.

5 REMOVE the risen dough from the bowl and transfer to a lightly floured surface. Knead well for about 2–3 minutes until the dough is smooth and silky. Divide into 30 pieces, then roll each piece into a long "sausage" shape, about 20cm/8in long. Arrange these on baking trays that have been lined with baking paper.

6 BRUSH lightly with the remaining olive oil, then sprinkle over the crushed sea salt. Bake in the preheated oven for 18–20 minutes until the breadsticks are golden brown. Allow to cool a little, then serve warm.

PART 2

THE RECIPES

*A traditional Italian meal has many components, from the **delicious** little antipasti **morsels**, often found in bars around the country and served with drinks at home, to simple **homemade** desserts. A meal would be incomplete without a pasta or risotto course, which is usually served as the first course or **primo piatto**, followed by a meat or fish course with some **simple** vegetables and salads.*

*In this chapter you will find a selection of **easy** recipes that characterize the **flavours** of the different Italian regions. Many may be familiar to you from your own **travels** and all of them can be easily reproduced in your own home.*

*The key to the success of all the recipes in this section is in the **quality** of the ingredients – for the best results it is always vital to use the **freshest** ingredients you can find. The **good** news is that all of the produce needed to prepare the recipes in this book is now widely **available**. But if you do have trouble sourcing an **ingredient** or finding the very best quality, do not worry about using a good substitute. The recipe may well be the **better** for it.*

CHARGRILLED VEGETABLE SALAD

INSALATA DI VERDURE GRIGLIATE

SERVES 4   PREPARATION TIME: 15 MINUTES   COOKING TIME: 20 MINUTES

The vibrant colours and flavours of this salad make it perfect for any weather.

250g/9oz fresh **asparagus**

3 **courgettes**

3 **peppers** (in a variety of colours)

1 large **aubergine**

3 tbsp **olive oil**

3 cloves **garlic**, crushed

salt and freshly ground **black pepper**

100g/3½oz **cherry tomatoes**

5 tbsp **extra-virgin olive oil**

2 tbsp **balsamic vinegar** *(see page 10)*

1 large handful **basil leaves**, roughly torn

1 TRIM off and discard any woody parts from the ends of the asparagus stems, then plunge them into a pan of boiling salted water for 2 minutes. Drain and rinse under cold running water to stop further cooking. Leave to dry on a piece of kitchen paper.

2 CUT the courgettes diagonally into 1cm/½in thick slices. Trim the peppers and cut into quarters, discarding the seeds and membrane. Slice the aubergine horizontally. Place all the prepared vegetables in a large bowl with the asparagus. Add the olive oil, 2 of the garlic cloves and salt and pepper to taste. Toss to coat the vegetables well.

3 HEAT a large griddle pan (see page 16) until hot and use to cook the vegetables until lightly browned and just soft. You may need to do this in batches, keeping cooked vegetables warm while preparing the remainder. Arrange on a large serving platter and top with the cherry tomatoes.

4 WHISK together the extra-virgin olive oil, balsamic vinegar and remaining garlic in a small bowl. Season to taste with salt and pepper, then pour over the vegetables and toss lightly. Scatter the basil leaves over the salad. Serve warm or at room temperature.

BAKED MUSSELS WITH CRISPY HERB BREADCRUMBS

COZZE GRATINATE

SERVES 4   PREPARATION TIME: 30 MINUTES   COOKING TIME: 5 MINUTES

The crunchiness of the topping in this dish works beautifully with the creamy softness of the mussels.

500g/1lb 2oz fresh **mussels**

7 tbsp dry **white wine**

1 clove **garlic**, chopped

3 tbsp **olive oil**

150g/5½oz fresh **white breadcrumbs**

1 large handful **flat-leaf parsley**, chopped

juice of 1 **lemon**, reserving ⅛ lemon wedge to serve

2 tbsp **extra-virgin olive oil**

freshly ground **black pepper**

1 CLEAN the mussels thoroughly by soaking in plenty of cold water. Use a sharp knife to remove any barnacles and the fibrous "beard" from the side of the mussels. Discard any with broken shells.

2 PLACE the mussels in a large saucepan and add the wine and garlic. Cover and cook over a high heat for 3–4 minutes. Strain off the liquid, discard any mussels that have not opened and leave to cool. Remove the mussels from their shells and set them on one side, along with half of the empty shells.

3 HEAT the olive oil in a large sauté pan (see page 17) and add the breadcrumbs. Stir well until lightly browned and then add the parsley.

4 PREHEAT the oven to 220°C/425°F/Gas 7. Place each mussel in a half-shell and top with some of the breadcrumb mixture. Arrange in a single layer in a shallow baking dish, drizzle over the lemon juice and extra-virgin olive oil, then bake in the hot oven for 5 minutes, until the breadcrumbs are golden. Season to taste with pepper and serve, accompanied by lemon wedge.

AUBERGINE WITH TOMATO SAUCE AND CHEESE

MELANZANE ALLA PARMIGIANA

SERVES **4–6** PREPARATION TIME: **25** MINUTES COOKING TIME: **20** MINUTES

Bursting with the fragrance of fresh tomatoes and basil, this makes a great appetizer as well as a good light lunch, served with a simple green salad.

4 large **aubergines**

5 tbsp **olive oil**

freshly ground **black pepper**

1 handful fresh **basil**, shredded

250g/9oz grated **mozzarella cheese**

1 recipe quantity **fresh tomato sauce**
(*see page 23*)

4 tbsp freshly grated **Parmesan cheese**

1 PREHEAT the oven to 200°C/400°F/Gas 6. Slice the aubergines into rounds, approximately 5mm/¼in thick. Brush both sides lightly with the olive oil and arrange in a single layer on a large baking tray. Season well with pepper.

2 BAKE in the hot oven for about 15 minutes, or until the aubergine is beginning to soften.

3 LAYER the baked aubergine in a lightly greased, ovenproof dish with the basil, mozzarella cheese and tomato sauce.

4 SPRINKLE over the Parmesan cheese and grind over black pepper to taste. Bake in the hot oven for 15–20 minutes until golden brown and bubbling. Leave to cool slightly before serving.

CROSTINI WITH GARLIC, TOMATO AND ANCHOVY

CROSTINI CON AGLIO, POMODORO E ACCIUGA

MAKES 24   PREPARATION TIME: 15 MINUTES   COOKING TIME: 10 MINUTES

These crispy little crostini make the perfect partner to pre-dinner drinks.
They can be served with different toppings (see page 42).

2 day-old **breadsticks** (*see page 31*)

2 tbsp **olive oil**

salt and freshly ground **black pepper**

TOPPING:

1 small clove **garlic**, crushed

2 medium **tomatoes**, peeled, deseeded and diced

1 **avocado**, diced

6 **anchovy** fillets (in salt), rinsed and diced

1 tsp **lemon juice**

1 tbsp **extra-virgin olive oil**

6 fresh **basil leaves**, roughly chopped

freshly ground **black pepper**

1 PREHEAT the oven to 180°C/350°F/Gas 4. Cut each breadstick into 12 slices and arrange in a single layer on a baking tray. Drizzle with the olive oil and season well with salt and pepper.

2 BAKE in the hot oven for about 10 minutes, until lightly browned. Remove the crostini from the oven and leave to cool slightly. (If not using immediately, they may be stored in an airtight tin and warmed briefly in the oven before topping and serving.)

3 PREPARE the topping by mixing together the garlic, tomatoes, avocado and anchovies in a bowl, then stir in the lemon juice, extra-virgin olive oil and basil leaves. Season to taste with black pepper.

4 PLACE a heaped teaspoon of the topping mixture on each of the warm crostini. Serve immediately.

CROSTINI WITH GORGONZOLA AND BLACK OLIVE TAPENADE

CROSTINI CON GORGONZOLA E PASTA D'OLIVE

MAKES 24   PREPARATION TIME: 15 MINUTES

The creaminess of the Gorgonzola contrasts wonderfully with the saltiness of the tapenade.

---

1 recipe quantity **crostini** *(see page 41)*

1 small clove **garlic**, cut in half

1 tbsp **extra-virgin olive oil**

150g/5½oz **Gorgonzola cheese**

4 tbsp **black olive tapenade** *(see page 20)*

1 **WARM** the crostini slightly in a hot oven, if not freshly baked. Then rub each one well with the cut surface of the garlic clove and drizzle over a little of the extra-virgin olive oil.

2 **SPREAD** 1 teaspoon of the Gorgonzola cheese over the top of each of the crostini, using a knife. Arrange on a serving platter.

3 **TOP** each of the crostini with a little of the black olive tapenade and serve immediately.

TUNA CARPACCIO

CARPACCIO DI TONNO

SERVES 4   PREPARATION TIME: 10 MINUTES, PLUS 1 HOUR FREEZING TIME

The tuna for this recipe must be of the highest quality and really fresh. Ask your fishmonger for the tail end of the tuna, as this is easier to slice. The softness of the tuna combined with the dressing is absolutely sublime.

300g/10oz piece fresh, top-quality **tuna** ("sashimi-grade")

juice and grated rind of 2 **lemons**

7 tbsp **extra-virgin olive oil**

1 clove **garlic**, crushed

2 tbsp **flat-leaf parsley**, finely chopped

salt and freshly ground **black pepper**

1 large handful **rocket**

2 tbsp **Parmesan cheese** shavings

1 PLACE the tuna in the freezer on a medium setting for about 1 hour, until it is firm but not hard.

2 MAKE a dressing by whisking together the lemon juice and rind, olive oil, garlic and parsley in a small bowl until well combined. Season to taste with salt and pepper.

3 REMOVE the tuna from the freezer and cut into very thin slices. Divide these equally between 4 serving plates. Drizzle a tablespoon of the dressing over each serving.

4 TOSS the remaining dressing with the rocket in a large bowl and place a little in the centre of each plate of tuna. Top with the Parmesan shavings and serve.

ASPARAGUS WITH BALSAMIC VINEGAR AND PARMESAN

ASPARAGI CON ACETO BALSAMICO E PARMIGIANO

SERVES 4   PREPARATION TIME: 20 MINUTES   COOKING TIME: 12 MINUTES

The addition of balsamic vinegar and Parmesan cheese really brings out the depth of flavour in the asparagus.

500g/1lb 2oz fresh **asparagus**, trimmed

2 tbsp **extra-virgin olive oil**

2 tbsp **balsamic vinegar** *(see page 10)*

2 tbsp **Parmesan cheese** shavings

freshly ground **black pepper**

1 **PREHEAT** the oven to 220°C/425°F/Gas 7.

2 **TOSS** the asparagus with 1 tablespoon of the extra-virgin olive oil and place on a baking tray that has been lined with baking paper. Bake in the hot oven for about 10–12 minutes, until the asparagus is just tender. Remove from the oven.

3 **PLACE** the asparagus on a serving dish and drizzle over the balsamic vinegar and remaining olive oil. Top with the parmesan shavings and freshly ground black pepper to taste. Serve warm.

PIEDMONT ROAST PEPPERS

PEPERONI ARROSTI ALLA PIEMONTESE

SERVES 4 PREPARATION TIME: 15 MINUTES COOKING TIME: 35 MINUTES

These peppers are full of tangy flavours and they also look spectacular.

---

4 **red peppers**, halved lengthways

200g/7oz **cherry tomatoes**

16 stuffed **green olives**

8 **anchovy** fillets, rinsed

1 clove **garlic**, very thinly sliced

1 tbsp **capers**, rinsed

40g/1½oz **butter**

2 tbsp **extra-virgin olive oil**

1 small handful fresh **basil**, roughly chopped

1 PREHEAT the oven to 200°C/400°F/Gas 6.

2 REMOVE all the membranes and seeds from the halved peppers and arrange them on a lightly greased baking tray, cut side up.

3 DIVIDE the cherry tomatoes, olives, anchovy fillets, garlic and capers evenly between each half of pepper. Top each with a small knob of butter and drizzle over the extra-virgin olive oil.

4 BAKE in the hot oven for 30–35 minutes, until the peppers are soft but still hold their shape. Leave to cool for about 5 minutes, then sprinkle over the fresh basil and serve.

COURGETTE FRITTATA

FRITTATA CON LE ZUCCHINE

SERVES 4   PREPARATION TIME: 15 MINUTES   COOKING TIME: 15 MINUTES

The eggs should be cooked until they are just beginning to set. This will give the dish a lovely creamy consistency and allow the full flavour of the other ingredients to shine through.

25g/1oz **butter**

1 **onion**, diced

2 **courgettes**, diced

2 **potatoes**, peeled, cooked and cut into small chunks

5 **eggs**

1 large handful **flat-leaf parsley**, chopped

1 small handful **basil leaves**, shredded

6 tbsp freshly grated **Parmesan cheese**

salt and freshly ground **black pepper**

1 MELT the butter in a large, non-stick frying pan. Add the onion and cook over a very low heat for 2–3 minutes, until soft but not brown.

2 ADD the diced courgettes and cook for another 2–3 minutes, until just soft, then add the potatoes and cook for a further 1 minute.

3 BEAT together the eggs, parsley, basil and Parmesan cheese in a large bowl and season to taste with salt and pepper. Pour over the vegetable mixture in the pan and leave to cook over a low heat for around 5 minutes, until the egg mixture has set around the sides but is still liquid in the centre, then remove from the heat. Meanwhile, preheat the grill until very hot.

4 PLACE the frittata, still in the frying pan, under the hot grill briefly to brown the top. Serve warm or cold, cut into 4 individual portions.

ANCHOVY AND GARLIC DIP

BAGNA CAUDA

SERVES 4   PREPARATION TIME: 30 MINUTES   COOKING TIME: 5 MINUTES

This warm dip is deliciously salty and tastes brilliant with freshly prepared vegetable crudités.

10 tbsp **olive oil**

6 cloves **garlic**, crushed

125g/4oz **anchovy** fillets, finely chopped

100g/3½oz **butter**, diced

assorted **vegetable crudités**, such as sticks of carrots and celery, trimmed radishes and small florets of blanched broccoli, freshly prepared

1 WARM the olive oil, garlic and anchovies in a small saucepan over a low heat, stirring well to combine. Leave to cook for 4–5 minutes, stirring occasionally, until the anchovies form a paste, but do not allow the garlic to brown.

2 REMOVE from the heat and stir in the butter until it has melted.

3 POUR the dip into a bowl and serve warm with the fresh crudités.

WILD MUSHROOM AND SHALLOT TARTS

TORTE DI FUNGHI E SCALOGNO

SERVES 4   PREPARATION TIME: 45 MINUTES   COOKING TIME: 10 MINUTES

The richness of the mushrooms and the crispness of the pastry make a heavenly match.

200g/7oz **plain flour**

4 tbsp freshly grated **Parmesan cheese**

salt and freshly ground **black pepper**

125g/4½oz **butter**, diced

1 **egg yolk**

3 tbsp **olive oil**

8 **shallots**, finely chopped

1 **red onion**, diced

100g/3½oz **pancetta**, diced

1 clove **garlic**, crushed

400g/14oz mixed **wild mushrooms**, sliced

100ml/3½fl oz/½ cup **red wine**

1 large handful **flat-leaf parsley**, chopped

2 handfuls **rocket**

1 MIX the flour, Parmesan cheese and black pepper to taste in a large bowl. Rub in 100g/3½oz butter with your fingertips until the mixture resembles fine breadcrumbs. Mix in the egg yolk with enough cold water to form a soft ball of pastry.

2 ROLL out and use to line 4 x 10cm/4in loose-bottom tart tins. Place a piece of baking paper in each and top with a handful of baking beans. Chill in the fridge for 30 minutes. Preheat the oven to 200°C/400°F/Gas 6.

3 BAKE the tart cases in the hot oven for about 15 minutes, until just starting to brown. Remove the paper and baking beans, then bake for a further 10 minutes, until golden brown. Turn out of the tins and set aside.

4 HEAT the oil in a large pan. Add the shallots and cook until lightly browned. Remove from the pan and set aside. Add the onion and sauté for 2–3 minutes, until soft. Toss in the pancetta and garlic and cook for 2 minutes, then add the mushrooms and cook for 3 minutes. Return the shallots to the pan with the wine and allow to bubble briefly. Whisk in the remaining butter and the parsley and season to taste with salt and pepper.

5 WARM the tart cases in the oven. Divide the mushroom mixture between them and serve immediately with a garnish of rocket.

DEEP-FRIED RICE BALLS

SUPPLÌ

MAKES 20   PREPARATION TIME: 40 MINUTES, PLUS 1 HOUR COOLING TIME
COOKING TIME: 10 MINUTES

*The crisp, outer coating of these warm rice balls makes a lovely contrast
to their soft, creamy centre.*

---

1 litre/1¾ pints/4 cups **chicken** or **vegetable
stock** *(see page 18 or 19)*

25g/1oz **butter**

1 clove **garlic**, crushed

250g/9oz **risotto rice** *(see page 14)*

5 tbsp **double cream**

55g/2oz freshly grated **Parmesan cheese**

salt and freshly ground **black pepper**

250g/9oz **mozzarella cheese**, cut into
approximately 20 small cubes

2 **eggs**, lightly beaten

breadcrumbs, for coating

vegetable oil, for deep-frying

1 recipe quantity **fresh tomato sauce**
(see page 23), **to serve**

1 HEAT the stock in a large pan until just beginning to bubble. Lower
the heat and keep at a low simmer.

2 MELT the butter in a medium saucepan over a low heat. Add the
garlic and cook for 1 minute. Add the risotto rice and cook, stirring, for
a further minute. Add a ladleful of the hot stock and continue cooking,
stirring constantly, until it has been absorbed. Continue adding the
stock in this way until the rice is tender. (It may not be necessary to add
all the stock.) As soon as the rice is cooked, stir in the cream.

3 REMOVE from the heat, stir in the Parmesan cheese and season to
taste with salt and pepper. Spread out on a baking tray and leave to cool.

4 SHAPE spoonfuls of the cold rice mixture into balls, large enough to
encase a cube of the mozzarella, placed in the centre. Roll each ball in
the beaten egg, then in the breadcrumbs, until well coated.

5 POUR enough oil into a pan to deep-fry the rice balls. Heat until hot
enough to brown a cube of day-old bread in about 30 seconds. Deep-fry
the prepared rice balls, in batches of 4–5, until crisp and golden. Drain
on kitchen paper and serve warm with the tomato sauce for dipping.

BRUSCHETTA WITH TOMATO AND BASIL

BRUSCHETTA CON POMODORO E BASILICO

SERVES 4   PREPARATION TIME: 20 MINUTES   COOKING TIME: 5 MINUTES

Ripe tomatoes and fresh basil create the perfect flavour combination.

8 slices **ciabatta bread**, about 1cm/½in thick

1 clove **garlic**, cut in half

4 tbsp **extra-virgin olive oil**

4 **tomatoes**, finely chopped

1 small handful **basil leaves**, torn

salt and freshly ground **black pepper**

1 TOAST the ciabatta slices under a hot grill until golden brown on both sides.

2 RUB each piece of toast all over with the cut side of the garlic while still warm, then drizzle each with a little olive oil. Set on one side.

3 MIX together the chopped tomatoes and torn basil in a bowl and season to taste with salt and pepper.

4 PLACE one or two spoonfuls of the tomato mixture on top of each piece of toast and serve.

THICK VEGETABLE SOUP WITH PESTO

MINESTRONE ALLA GENOVESE

SERVES 4 PREPARATION TIME: 25 MINUTES, PLUS 8 HOURS SOAKING TIME
COOKING TIME: 2 HOURS

150g/5½oz dried **borlotti beans**

3 tbsp **olive oil**

1 large **onion**, sliced

2 sticks **celery**, sliced

1 **carrot**, sliced

2 cloves **garlic**, crushed

100g/3½oz thickly sliced **pancetta**, diced

1 tbsp **tomato purée**

1 litre/1¾ pints/4 cups **chicken** or **vegetable stock** *(see page 18 or 19)*

1 x 400g/14oz tin chopped **tomatoes**

2 **potatoes**, peeled and diced

100g/3½oz shelled fresh **peas**

1 **courgette**, diced

100g/3½oz **green beans**, roughly chopped

1 handful **flat-leaf parsley**, roughly chopped

salt and freshly ground **black pepper**

basil pesto *(see page 24)* and freshly grated **Parmesan cheese**, to serve

1 PLACE the borlotti beans in a large pan. Cover with cold water and leave to soak for 8 hours or overnight. Drain, rinse several times in cold water and set aside.

2 HEAT the olive oil in a large saucepan over a moderate heat. Add the onion, celery and carrot and cook for 3–4 minutes, stirring frequently. Add the garlic and pancetta and cook for another 2 minutes, then stir in the tomato purée until well combined.

3 STIR the drained beans into the pan of vegetables, along with the stock and the chopped tomatoes. Lower the heat and leave to simmer for about 1½ hours, until the borlotti beans begin to soften.

4 ADD the potatoes, peas, courgette, green beans and parsley and continue to simmer for a further 30 minutes, until the vegetables are tender.

5 SEASON to taste with salt and freshly ground pepper and serve in warm bowls, with a spoonful of pesto and a sprinkling of freshly grated Parmesan cheese added just before serving.

VENETIAN PEA AND RICE SOUP

RISI E BISI

SERVES 4   PREPARATION TIME: 20 MINUTES   COOKING TIME: 20 MINUTES

This is a cross between a thick soup and a risotto. You could almost think of it as a "lazy" risotto, as it does not require constant stirring.

1 litre/1¾ pints/4 cups **chicken** or **vegetable stock** *(see page 18 or 19)*

2 tbsp **olive oil**

60g/2¼oz **butter**

1 small **onion**, diced

55g/2oz thickly sliced **pancetta**, diced

150g/5½oz **risotto rice** *(see page 14)*

300g/10½oz shelled fresh **peas**

1 small handful fresh **mint**, roughly chopped

4 tbsp freshly grated **Parmesan cheese**

salt and freshly ground **black pepper**

1 HEAT the stock in a saucepan until just bubbling. Keep at a gentle simmer. In a large, clean pan heat the olive oil with half the butter. Add the onion and cook over a low heat for about 5 minutes, stirring often, until soft and translucent.

2 ADD the pancetta and cook a further 2 minutes over a medium heat, then add the rice and stir to coat well with the butter mixture.

3 POUR in the hot stock, lower the heat and leave to simmer for about 10 minutes, stirring occasionally.

4 ADD the peas and cook for a further 5–6 minutes, until they are tender. Remove from the heat, then stir in the remaining butter, the mint and the Parmesan cheese. Season to taste with salt and pepper and serve immediately.

WINTER VEGETABLE SOUP

LA RIBOLLITA

SERVES 4   PREPARATION TIME: 20 MINUTES   COOKING TIME: 30 MINUTES

This soup is rich and satisfying – just perfect for a midwinter treat.

3 tbsp **olive oil**

1 **onion**, diced

1 large **carrot**, diced

2 sticks **celery**, diced

3 **courgettes**, diced

2 cloves **garlic**, crushed

1.2 litres/2 pints/4¾ cups **chicken** or **vegetable stock** *(see page 18 or 19)*

300g/10½oz **cavolo nero**, finely sliced *(see page 15)*

250g/9oz fresh **white breadcrumbs**

salt and freshly ground **black pepper**

extra-virgin olive oil, to serve

1 HEAT the olive oil in a large saucepan. Add the onion and cook over a low heat for 2–3 minutes, until soft. Add the carrot, celery and courgettes and cook a further 5 minutes, then stir in the garlic and cook for another minute.

2 ADD the stock and cavolo nero and bring to the boil. Lower the heat, stir in the breadcrumbs and leave to simmer gently for around 30 minutes, until the vegetables are tender.

3 SEASON to taste with salt and pepper. Serve in warm bowls with a little extra-virgin olive oil drizzled over the top.

FISH SOUP

ZUPPA DI PESCE

SERVES 4   PREPARATION TIME: 25 MINUTES   COOKING TIME: 30 MINUTES

This intensely flavoured seafood broth is light and refreshing.

200g/7oz raw **prawns**, shelled

150g/5½oz **monkfish** fillets,
    membrane removed

150g/5½oz **cod**

150g/5½oz shelled **scallops**, roe removed

3 tbsp **olive oil**

1 small stick **celery**, finely diced

1 **carrot**, finely diced

1 bulb **fennel**, finely diced

2 cloves **garlic**, crushed

10 tbsp dry **white wine**

1 x 400g/14oz tin **chopped tomatoes**

1 litre/1¾ pints/4 cups **fish stock** *(see page 19)*

salt and freshly ground **black pepper**

1 handful **flat-leaf parsley**, roughly chopped

1 **PEEL** the prawns and cut the monkfish, cod and scallops into bite-sized pieces. Set aside in the fridge until required.

2 **HEAT** the oil in a large saucepan. Add the celery, carrot and fennel and cook over a medium heat for around 5 minutes, stirring often to prevent browning. Add the garlic and cook another 1 minute.

3 **POUR** in the white wine, chopped tomatoes and fish stock and bring to the boil. Reduce the heat and leave to simmer for 25 minutes.

4 **STIR** in the prepared fish and continue to simmer for a further 5 minutes. Season to taste with salt and pepper and stir in the chopped parsley. Serve immediately.

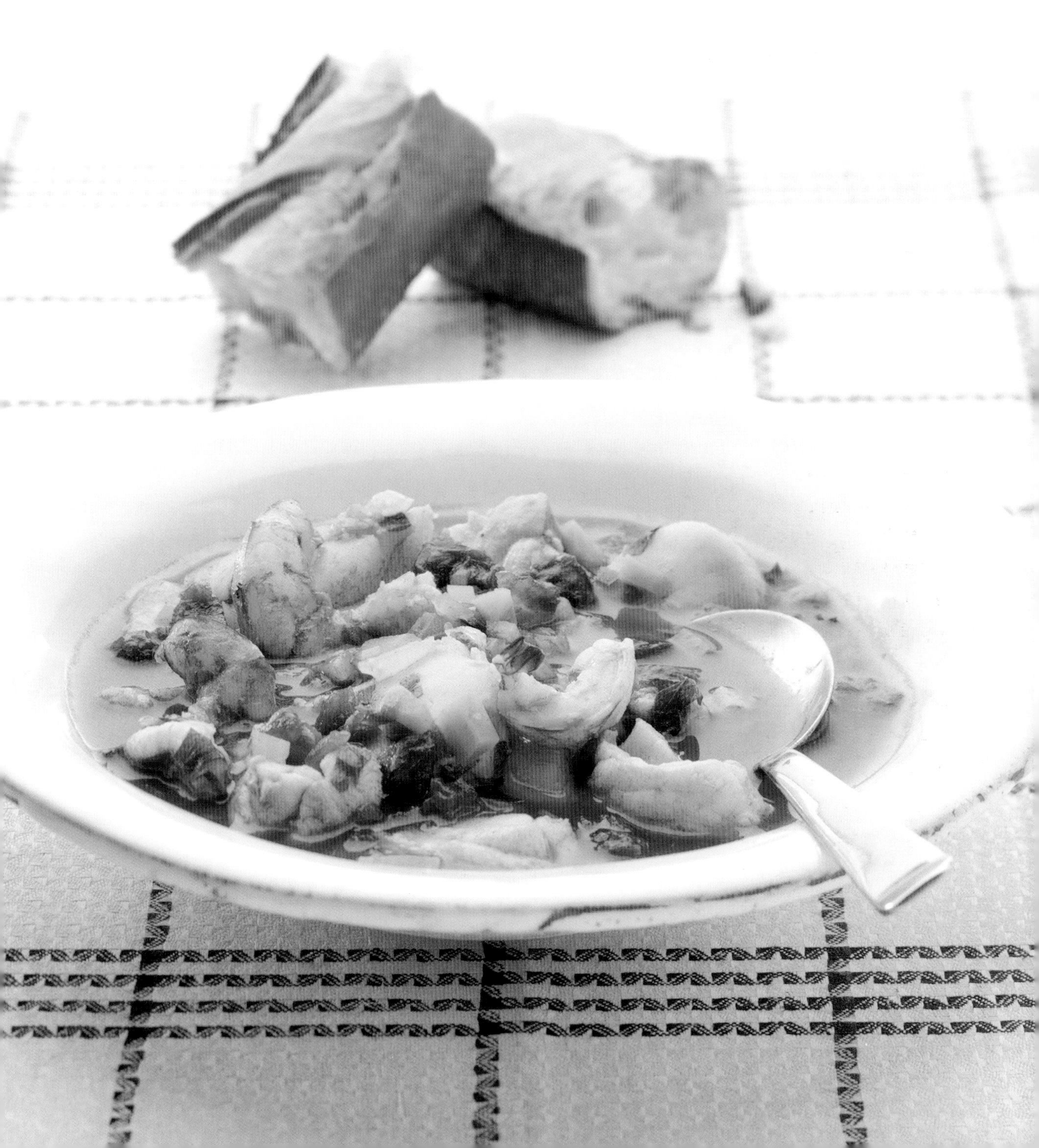

PASTA AND BEAN SOUP

PASTA E FAGIOLI

SERVES 4   PREPARATION TIME: 20 MINUTES, PLUS 8 HOURS SOAKING TIME
COOKING TIME: 1½ HOURS

This is a typical rustic Italian soup. The swirl of olive oil, added on the top just before serving, helps to enhance the flavour.

300g/10½oz dried **borlotti beans**

2 sprigs fresh **rosemary**

1 tbsp **olive oil**

1 **onion**, diced

2 cloves **garlic**, peeled

1.5 litres/2¾ pints/6 cups **chicken** or **vegetable stock** *(see page 18 or 19)*

2 handfuls **flat-leaf parsley**, roughly chopped

salt and freshly ground **black pepper**

100g/3½oz short **pasta tubes**

extra-virgin olive oil, to serve

1 PLACE the borlotti beans in a large pan. Cover with cold water and leave to soak for 8 hours or overnight.

2 DRAIN the beans and rinse thoroughly. Place in a clean pan and cover with plenty of fresh cold water. Add the rosemary and bring to the boil. Simmer for about 1 hour or until tender. Drain and set on one side.

3 HEAT the olive oil in a clean pan, add the onion and cook for about 5 minutes on a very low heat, stirring occasionally. Add the garlic and cook for another minute.

4 ADD the drained beans to the pan with the stock and about two-thirds of the parsley and season to taste with salt and pepper. Bring to the boil, lower the heat and leave to simmer for 30 minutes. Allow to cool a little.

5 TRANSFER to a blender or food processor and process until smooth (or use an immersion blender – see page 16). Return to the cleaned pan, add the pasta and cook for 10–12 minutes or until the pasta is tender. Season, if necessary, with salt and pepper.

6 DIVIDE between warm serving bowls. Serve topped with a swirl of extra-virgin olive oil and a sprinkling of the remaining parsley.

CREAMY TOMATO SOUP

PAPPA AL POMODORO

SERVES 4   PREPARATION TIME: 20 MINUTES   COOKING TIME: 5 MINUTES

This creamy tomato soup, with its vibrant flavour, originates in Tuscany. It is often served as a very thick, almost stew-like soup, although this version is much lighter.

3 tbsp olive oil

1 onion, sliced

2 cloves garlic, chopped

1kg/2lb 4oz ripe tomatoes, peeled, deseeded and chopped

4 tbsp fresh white breadcrumbs

1 small handful fresh basil leaves, torn

500ml/17fl oz/2 cups chicken stock *(see page 18)*

salt and freshly ground black pepper

1 HEAT the olive oil in a medium-sized saucepan. Add the onion and cook over a very low heat for 2–3 minutes, until soft. Add the garlic and cook for another minute.

2 STIR in the tomatoes and cook gently for about 3 minutes.

3 REMOVE from the heat and allow to cool slightly. Add the fresh breadcrumbs, basil and stock and transfer to a blender or food processor and process until smooth (or use an immersion blender, see page 16).

4 RETURN to the cleaned pan and heat through. Season to taste with salt and pepper and serve.

SPAGHETTI WITH PRAWNS

SPAGHETTI CON GAMBERETTI

SERVES 4   PREPARATION TIME: 10 MINUTES   COOKING TIME: 12 MINUTES

This simple yet elegant pasta dish is quick to prepare and packed with flavour.

400g/14oz dried **spaghetti**

2 tbsp **extra-virgin olive oil**

25g/1oz **butter**

1 small **onion**, finely diced

300g/10½oz raw **prawns**, shelled

3 **tomatoes**, diced

7 tbsp dry **white wine**

salt and freshly ground **black pepper**

1 small handful fresh **basil leaves**, torn

1 BRING a large pan of salted water to the boil. Add the spaghetti and cook, according to the packet instructions, until tender. Drain.

2 HEAT the olive oil and butter in another large saucepan while the pasta is cooking. Add the onion and cook, stirring frequently, for about 5 minutes, until soft.

3 ADD the prawns to the softened onion and continue cooking until they start to turn pink. Stir in the tomatoes and white wine, then season to taste with salt and pepper.

4 TOSS the prawn mixture and the basil with the freshly cooked pasta, until well mixed. Adjust the seasoning if needed and serve immediately.

SPAGHETTI WITH BREADCRUMBS

SPAGHETTI CON LA MOLLICA

SERVES **4**   PREPARATION TIME: **10** MINUTES   COOKING TIME: **12** MINUTES

The crunch of the breadcrumbs lends a surprising touch to this dish and adds a truly satisfying dimension to every mouthful.

5 tbsp **olive oil**

100g/3½oz **anchovies**, rinsed and drained

2 cloves **garlic**, crushed

100g/3½oz fresh **white breadcrumbs**

400g/14oz dried **spaghetti**

5 tbsp stoned **black olives**, sliced

1 tbsp **capers**, rinsed

juice and grated rind of 1 **lemon**

freshly ground **black pepper**

1 HEAT 2 tablespoons of olive oil in a small saucepan. Add the anchovies and cook until they form a paste. Add the garlic and cook for another minute. Set on one side.

2 HEAT the remaining oil in a large frying pan. Add the breadcrumbs and stir well to combine with the oil, then continue to cook until the breadcrumbs become golden brown. Remove from the heat and set aside.

3 COOK the spaghetti, according to the packet instructions, until tender, and drain.

4 MIX the freshly cooked pasta, the anchovy paste, breadcrumbs, olives, capers and lemon juice and rind. Season to taste with black pepper and serve immediately.

RIGATONI WITH ROASTED VEGETABLES

RIGATONI CON VERDURE ARROSTITE

SERVES 4 PREPARATION TIME: 15 MINUTES COOKING TIME: 40 MINUTES

The combination of roasted vegetables, fresh Parmesan and warm pasta makes a spectacular dish, fit for anything from a simple lunch to opener for a special dinner.

---

2 **carrots**, peeled

150g/5½oz **pumpkin**, peeled

2 **sweet potatoes**, peeled

1 **parsnip**, peeled

2 **courgettes**

5 tbsp **olive oil**

2 cloves **garlic**, sliced finely

1 small red **chilli**, deseeded and finely diced

2 sprigs **rosemary**, roughly chopped

salt and freshly ground **black pepper**

200g/7oz **cherry tomatoes**

400g/14oz dried **rigatoni pasta**

2 tbsp **extra-virgin olive oil**

1 large handful **flat-leaf parsley**, chopped

freshly grated **Parmesan cheese**, to serve

1 PREHEAT the oven to 180°C/350°F/Gas 4.

2 CUT the vegetables into roughly bite-sized chunks, making the carrots just a little smaller than the other vegetables. Place in a large bowl.

3 TOSS in the olive oil, garlic, chilli and rosemary, then season to taste with salt and pepper. Mix well until the vegetables are thoroughly coated in the seasoned oil. Arrange in a single layer on a baking tray.

4 ROAST the vegetables in the hot oven for about 20 minutes, until just starting to become tender. Add the tomatoes and cook for a further 10 minutes, until all the vegetables are cooked.

5 COOK the rigatoni in plenty of boiling salted water, according to the packet instructions, then drain.

6 TOSS the freshly cooked pasta with the extra-virgin olive oil, freshly roasted vegetables and chopped parsley. Serve immediately, with freshly grated Parmesan cheese.

THREE CHEESE RAVIOLI WITH BUTTER AND BASIL *RAVIOLI AI TRE FORMAGGI CON BURRO E BASILICO*

SERVES 4   PREPARATION TIME: 40 MINUTES   COOKING TIME: 10 MINUTES

The delicate flavour of these light pasta parcels is enhanced by the addition of extra-virgin olive oil, fragrant fresh basil and a dash of mouth-tingling lemon.

250g/9oz **ricotta cheese**

75g/2½oz freshly grated **pecorino cheese**

70g/2½oz freshly grated **Parmesan cheese**, plus extra for serving

1 small handful fresh **basil leaves**, shredded, plus extra for serving

salt and freshly ground **black pepper**

1 recipe quantity **fresh pasta** dough *(see page 26)*

1 tbsp **olive oil**

3 tbsp **extra-virgin olive oil**

25g/1oz **butter**, melted

juice and grated rind of 1 **lemon**

1 MIX the ricotta, pecorino and Parmesan cheeses with the basil in a bowl. Season with a little salt and plenty of pepper and set aside.

2 CUT the pasta dough into 4 pieces and roll out each one up to the second thinnest setting on the pasta machine. Lay 1 sheet of pasta on a well-floured surface and place 12 heaped teaspoons of the cheese mixture at equal intervals along it, allowing enough space around each to seal the ravioli. Brush around each heap of cheese mixture with a little water.

3 PLACE a second pasta sheet on top. Press down gently around the heaps of cheese filling to seal the 2 sheets of pasta together, making sure no excess air is trapped around the filling. With a sharp knife, cut into 12 individual ravioli. Repeat this process with the remaining 2 sheets of pasta to prepare 12 more ravioli.

4 BOIL a large saucepan of salted water. Add the tablespoon of olive oil, then the ravioli, and cook for about 5 minutes, until the pasta is tender but still has some bite. Carefully lift out of the water and drain using a slotted spoon. Divide between 4 warm serving plates.

5 MIX together the extra-virgin olive oil, melted butter and lemon juice and rind in a bowl and season to taste with pepper. Drizzle over the ravioli and serve with a sprinkling of shredded basil and grated Parmesan.

TAGLIATELLE WITH ASPARAGUS

TAGLIATELLE CON ASPARAGI

SERVES 4   PREPARATION TIME: 20 MINUTES   COOKING TIME: 12 MINUTES

The heat from the chilli helps to bring out all the flavours in this fabulous pasta dish.

500g/1lb 2oz fresh **asparagus**, trimmed

1 tbsp **olive oil**

1 small **onion**, diced

1 clove **garlic**, crushed

1 **red chilli**, deseeded and finely diced

3 **tomatoes**, peeled, deseeded and chopped

7 tbsp dry **white wine**

1 small handful **basil leaves**, shredded

1 large handful **flat-leaf parsley**, chopped

salt and freshly ground **black pepper**

400g/14oz fresh or dried **tagliatelle** *(see page 14)*

freshly grated **Parmesan cheese**, to serve

1 PLUNGE the asparagus into a pan of boiling water for 1 minute, then drain and rinse thoroughly under cold running water to cool. Cut into approximately 1cm/½in lengths on the diagonal and set on one side.

2 HEAT the olive oil in a large sauté pan (see page 17). Add the onion and cook over a medium heat for 3–5 minutes, until soft and slightly golden. Add the asparagus, garlic and chilli and continue cooking for another 3–4 minutes.

3 POUR in the tomatoes and white wine and bring to the boil. Lower the heat and simmer gently for 5 minutes. Stir in the basil and parsley. Season to taste with salt and pepper, then set aside and keep warm.

4 COOK the pasta in a large pan of boiling salted water until just tender. Drain, then toss with the warm sauce and serve, sprinkled with freshly grated Parmesan cheese.

"ANGRY" PASTA

PENNE ALL'ARRABBIATA

SERVES 4   PREPARATION TIME: 15 MINUTES   COOKING TIME: 20 MINUTES

This dish is typically served very hot and spicy, hence its name. But you can make it as mild or as fiery as you prefer, by increasing or decreasing the number of chillies you use when preparing the sauce.

2 tbsp **olive oil**

1 **onion**, sliced

2 **red chillies**, deseeded and finely diced

200g/7oz thickly sliced **pancetta**, diced

1 clove **garlic**, crushed

2 x 400g/14oz tins chopped **tomatoes**

7 tbsp dry **white wine**

400g/14oz dried **penne pasta**

1 handful **flat-leaf parsley**, chopped roughly

freshly shaved or grated **Parmesan cheese**, to serve

1 HEAT the oil in a large sauté pan (see page 17). Add the onion and cook over a moderate heat for 3 minutes, stirring often to prevent browning. Add the chilli, pancetta and garlic and continue cooking for another 2 minutes.

2 STIR in the tomatoes and white wine. Lower the heat and leave to simmer for 15 minutes, until the sauce has thickened. Set on one side and keep warm.

3 COOK the penne in plenty of boiling salted water, according to the packet instructions, until it is tender but still retains some bite. Drain and toss with the warm sauce and the chopped parsley. Serve with the Parmesan cheese.

BAKED LASAGNE

LASAGNE AL FORNO

SERVES 4—6 PREPARATION TIME: 35 MINUTES, PLUS 2—3 HOURS
COOKING TIME FOR SAUCE COOKING TIME: 40—45 MINUTES

Nothing beats the flavour of a traditional, homemade lasagne. The layers should be distinct and oozing with rich warming ragù sauce and creamy béchamel.

4 tbsp **olive oil**

1 **onion**, diced

1 **carrot**, finely diced

2 sticks **celery**, finely diced

100g/3½oz thickly sliced **pancetta**, diced

500g/1lb 2oz lean minced **beef**

500g/1lb 2oz minced **veal**

250ml/9fl oz/1 cup **milk**

250ml/9fl oz/1 cup **white wine**

1 x 400g/14oz tin chopped **tomatoes**

1 x 500g/1lb 2oz jar **passata** *(see page 14)*

500ml/17fl oz/2 cups **water**

salt and freshly ground **black pepper**

1 recipe quantity **fresh pasta** sheets *(see page 26)*

1 recipe quantity **béchamel sauce** *(see page 20)*

4 tbsp freshly grated **Parmesan cheese**

1 HEAT the olive oil in a large pan over a low heat. Add the onion and cook for 2—3 minutes, until soft. Add the carrot and celery, and cook for another 2 minutes.

2 TURN up the heat, add the pancetta and cook, stirring, for 1 minute. Add the beef and veal and cook until the meat has browned. Pour in the milk and allow to boil vigorously until all the liquid has evaporated.

3 ADD the wine, tomatoes and passata and turn the heat down to very low. Pour in the water and season to taste with salt and pepper. Simmer very gently for about 2—3 hours to let the flavours fully develop, adding extra water if required to prevent the sauce becoming too dry. Set on one side to cool until needed. Preheat the oven to 180°C/350°F/Gas 4.

4 CUT the fresh pasta sheets into pieces that will fit the base of an ovenproof dish, approximately 26cm/10½in by 20cm/8in. Layer the pasta with the meat sauce and béchamel sauce into the dish, starting with a layer of pasta and ending with a layer of béchamel. Sprinkle the Parmesan cheese over the top.

5 BAKE in the hot oven for 40—45 minutes, until lightly browned and bubbling. Serve.

SPAGHETTI CARBONARA

SPAGHETTI ALLA CARBONARA

SERVES 4   PREPARATION TIME: 10 MINUTES   COOKING TIME: 12 MINUTES

This perennially popular recipe originated in the Lazio region of Italy, which has Rome at its centre, but it can now be found all over Italy.

2 **eggs**

2 tbsp freshly grated **Parmesan cheese**, plus extra to serve

2 tbsp freshly grated **pecorino cheese**

1 tbsp **olive oil**

25g/1oz **butter**

1 clove **garlic**, crushed

175g/6oz thickly sliced **pancetta**, diced

400g/14oz dried **spaghetti**

salt and freshly ground **black pepper**

1 WHISK together the eggs, Parmesan and pecorino in a bowl and set on one side.

2 HEAT the olive oil and butter in a frying pan. Add the garlic and pancetta and cook over a medium heat until the pancetta is crisp and the garlic is golden brown. Discard the garlic and set the pancetta aside.

3 COOK the spaghetti in plenty of salted boiling water, according to the instructions on the packet, until tender but still retaining some bite.

4 DRAIN the pasta, then return it to the pan. Toss in the egg mixture and the cooked pancetta and combine well. Season to taste with salt and pepper and serve immediately, with extra grated Parmesan sprinkled over the top if desired.

SPINACH AND RICOTTA RAVIOLI

RAVIOLI DI RICOTTA E SPINACI

SERVES 4   PREPARATION TIME: 40 MINUTES   COOKING TIME: 10 MINUTES

*With their subtle flavourings of ricotta cheese, spinach and nutmeg,
these traditional ravioli are mouth-wateringly delicious.*

400g/14oz fresh **spinach**, rinsed thoroughly

25g/1oz **butter**

1 small **onion**, diced

2 tbsp grated **Parmesan cheese**,
    plus extra for serving

250g/9oz **ricotta cheese**

½ tsp freshly grated **nutmeg**

salt and freshly ground **black pepper**

1 recipe quantity **fresh pasta** dough *(see page 26)*

85g/3oz **butter**, melted

1 COOK the spinach in a small amount of boiling water until just wilted. Drain, squeeze out as much water as possible, chop finely and set aside.

2 MELT the butter in a pan over a low heat. Add the onion and cook for 3–4 minutes until soft. Off the heat, stir in the spinach, Parmesan, ricotta and nutmeg. Season to taste with salt and pepper and set aside.

3 CUT the pasta dough into 4 pieces and roll out each one up to the second thinnest setting on the pasta machine. Lay 1 pasta sheet on a floured surface and place 12 heaped teaspoons of the spinach mixture at equal intervals along it, allowing enough space around each to seal the ravioli. Brush around each heap of spinach mixture with a little water.

4 PLACE a second pasta sheet on top. Press down gently around the heaps of filling to seal the 2 sheets of pasta together, ensuring no excess air is trapped around the filling. With a sharp knife, cut into 12 individual ravioli. Repeat with the remaining pasta sheets and filling.

5 BOIL a large saucepan of salted water. Add the ravioli and cook for 5 minutes, or until the pasta is just tender. Lift out of the pan and drain, using a slotted spoon, then divide between 4 warm serving plates.

6 DRIZZLE the melted butter over the top of the ravioli, sprinkle with some freshly grated Parmesan cheese and serve.

POTATO GNOCCHI WITH BASIL, MOZZARELLA AND ROASTED CHERRY TOMATOES *GNOCCHI DI PATATE*

SERVES 4   PREPARATION TIME: 40 MINUTES   COOKING TIME: 5 MINUTES

Using a potato ricer will produce the lightest possible gnocchi. If you do not have one, however, you can simply mash them.

200g/7oz **cherry tomatoes**

1 tbsp **olive oil**

1kg/2lb 4oz **potatoes**, wrapped in foil and baked in the oven until very soft

200g/7oz **plain flour**

1 **egg**, lightly beaten

salt and freshly ground **black pepper**

3 tbsp **basil pesto** *(see page 24)*

1 small handful baby **mozzarella cheeses**, halved

freshly grated **Parmesan cheese**, to serve

1 PREHEAT the oven to 200°C/400°F/Gas 6. Arrange the cherry tomatoes on a baking tray, sprinkle over the olive oil and cook in the hot oven until just soft. Set on one side.

2 SCOOP the flesh out of the potatoes, discarding the skins, and press through a potato ricer (or simply mash). Place in a large bowl with the flour and egg and stir to combine. Season to taste with salt and pepper, then tip onto a floured surface and knead to form a soft, pliable dough.

3 SHAPE the dough into long cylinders approximately 1.5cm/⅔in in diameter, then cut each one into 2cm/¾in lengths. Mark these gnocchi lengths lightly with the back of a fork, then arrange on a tray that has been lightly dusted with flour.

4 BRING a large pan of salted water to the boil. Add the gnocchi and cook for about 5 minutes, or until the gnocchi rise to the top of the water. Lift out of the pan and drain, using a slotted spoon.

5 PLACE the hot gnocchi in a large bowl with the pesto, mozzarella and cherry tomatoes and toss gently to combine. Serve immediately, sprinkled with freshly grated Parmesan cheese.

SEMOLINA GNOCCHI WITH FRESH TOMATO SAUCE

GNOCCHI ALLA ROMANA

SERVES 4–6 PREPARATION TIME: 20 MINUTES, PLUS 1 HOUR COOLING TIME
COOKING TIME: 20 MINUTES

This is real comfort food. Just serve with a simple green salad.

1 litre/1¾ pints/4 cups **milk**

salt and freshly ground **black pepper**

250g/9oz **semolina**

2 **egg yolks**

200g/7oz **Parmesan cheese**, freshly grated

100g/3½oz **butter**, chopped

1 recipe quantity **fresh tomato sauce**
  (see page 23)

1 HEAT the milk in a saucepan with a little salt and pepper until it is just starting to boil.

2 WHISK in the semolina, then cook for about 10 minutes over a low heat, stirring constantly with a wooden spoon, until the mixture becomes quite thick.

3 REMOVE from the heat and add the egg yolks, half the Parmesan cheese and half the butter.

4 SPREAD the mixture over a large baking tray, lined with greaseproof paper, to a depth of about 1cm/½in. Leave to cool for 1 hour.

5 PREHEAT the oven to 200°C/400°F/Gas 6. Grease an ovenproof dish with a little of the remaining butter.

6 CUT circles out from the cooled gnocchi mixture, using a biscuit cutter, and arrange in a single layer in the greased dish. Dot with the remaining butter. Spoon over the tomato sauce and sprinkle over the remaining Parmesan cheese.

7 BAKE the gnocchi in the hot oven for about 20 minutes, until golden brown and bubbling. Serve immediately.

SAFFRON RISOTTO

RISOTTO ALLA MILANESE

SERVES 4   PREPARATION TIME: 10 MINUTES   COOKING TIME: 20 MINUTES

The saffron gives this risotto a rich yellow colour and intense flavour.

---

1 litre/1¾ pints/4 cups **chicken** or **vegetable stock** *(see page 18 or 19)*

85g/3oz **butter**

1 small **onion**, diced

300g/10½oz **risotto rice** *(see page 14)*

125ml/4fl oz/½ cup **white wine**

¼ tsp **saffron threads**, soaked in 2 tbsp boiling water for 10 minutes, water reserved

4 tbsp freshly grated **Parmesan cheese**, plus extra for serving

salt and freshly ground **black pepper**

1 HEAT the stock over a medium heat until just beginning to boil. Lower the heat and leave to simmer very gently.

2 MELT 60g/2oz of the butter in another saucepan. Add the onion and cook over a low heat for around 5 minutes, until soft but not brown.

3 ADD the rice and toast for 2 minutes, stirring constantly, then add the white wine and stir until it has evaporated. Add a ladleful of the hot stock and cook, stirring constantly, until it has all been absorbed by the rice. Continue in this way, adding the saffron and its soaking liquid after the first 10 minutes of cooking, until the rice is just tender but still retains some bite and is creamy in consistency. (It may not be necessary to use all the stock.)

4 STIR in the remaining butter and the Parmesan cheese and season to taste with salt and pepper. Leave to stand, covered, for 1–2 minutes, then serve with extra freshly grated Parmesan cheese.

ASPARAGUS RISOTTO

RISOTTO CON ASPARAGI

SERVES 4   PREPARATION TIME: 10 MINUTES   COOKING TIME: 20 MINUTES

The freshness of the asparagus combines superbly with the creaminess of the risotto rice in this truly sublime dish.

500g/1lb 2oz **green asparagus**, trimmed

1 litre/1¾ pints/4 cups **chicken** or **vegetable stock** *(see page 18 or 19)*

85g/3oz **butter**

1 small **onion**, finely diced

300g/10½oz **risotto rice** *(see page 14)*

4 tbsp freshly grated **Parmesan cheese**, plus extra for serving (optional)

salt and freshly ground **black pepper**

1 COOK the asparagus in a pan of boiling salted water until just starting to soften. Drain, rinse under cold running water to cool, then pat dry on kitchen paper. Cut into bite-sized chunks and set on one side.

2 HEAT the stock over a medium heat until just beginning to boil. Lower the heat and leave to simmer very gently.

3 MELT 60g/2¼oz of the butter in another saucepan. Add the onion and cook over a low heat for 3–4 minutes, until soft but not brown.

4 STIR in the rice and allow to toast for 2 minutes, then add a ladleful of the hot stock and cook, stirring constantly, until it has all been absorbed by the rice. Continue in this way, adding hot stock and stirring, until the rice is just tender but still retains some bite and is creamy in consistency. (It may not be necessary to use all the stock.)

5 STIR in the asparagus, the remaining butter and the Parmesan cheese and adjust the seasoning if necessary. Leave to stand, covered, for 1–2 minutes, then serve with extra freshly grated Parmesan cheese sprinkled over the top, if desired.

MUSHROOM RISOTTO

RISOTTO AI FUNGHI

SERVES 4   PREPARATION TIME: 10 MINUTES   COOKING TIME: 20 MINUTES

Risotto makes a great meal at any time and one of the best ways of flavouring it is by cooking it with wild mushrooms.

400g/14oz mixed **wild mushrooms** *(see page 12)*

150g/5½oz **butter**

1 litre/1¾ pints/4 cups **chicken** or **vegetable stock** *(see page 18 or 19)*

1 small **onion**, diced

300g/10½oz **risotto rice** *(see page 14)*

4 tbsp freshly grated **Parmesan cheese**, plus extra for serving (optional)

salt and freshly ground **black pepper**

1 WIPE the mushrooms thoroughly and slice thinly. Heat 50g/1¾oz of the butter in a sauté pan (see page 17) and cook the mushrooms for about 4–5 minutes, until soft. Remove from the pan and set aside.

2 HEAT the stock over a medium heat until just beginning to boil. Lower the heat and leave to simmer very gently.

3 MELT 60g/2¼oz of the butter in another saucepan. Add the onion and cook over a low heat for 3–4 minutes, until soft but not brown.

4 STIR in the rice and allow to toast for 2 minutes, then add a ladleful of the hot stock and cook, stirring constantly, until it has all been absorbed by the rice. Continue in this way, adding hot stock and stirring, until the rice is just tender but still retains some bite and is creamy in consistency. (It may not be necessary to use all the stock.)

5 STIR in the mushrooms, the remaining butter and Parmesan cheese and adjust the seasoning if necessary. Leave to stand, covered, for 1–2 minutes, then serve with extra freshly grated Parmesan cheese sprinkled over the top, if desired.

RISOTTO WITH PRAWNS AND CHAMPAGNE

RISOTTO ALLO CHAMPAGNE CON GAMBERETTI

SERVES 4 PREPARATION TIME: 15 MINUTES COOKING TIME: 20 MINUTES

Make this for a special celebration meal, or anytime you feel indulgent.

200g/7oz raw **prawns**, shelled

750ml/1½ pints/3 cups **fish stock** *(see page 19)*

85g/3oz **butter**

1 small **onion**, finely diced

1 clove **garlic**, crushed

300g/10½oz **risotto rice** *(see page 14)*

200ml/7fl oz/¾ cup **Champagne**

salt and freshly ground **black pepper**

1 RINSE the prawns, cut in half horizontally and keep refrigerated until required.

2 HEAT the stock over a medium heat until just beginning to boil. Lower the heat and leave to simmer very gently.

3 MELT 60g/2¼oz of the butter in another saucepan. Add the onion and garlic and cook over a low heat for 3–4 minutes, until soft but not brown.

4 ADD the rice and toast for 1 minute, stirring constantly, then pour over half of the Champagne and keep stirring until it has evaporated.

5 POUR in a ladleful of the hot stock and cook, stirring constantly, until it has all been absorbed by the rice. Continue in this way, adding hot stock and stirring, until the rice is just tender but still retains some bite and has a creamy consistency. (It may not be necessary to use all the stock.)

6 TOSS in the prawns and cook a further minute until they turn pink. Stir in the remaining Champagne and butter and season to taste with salt and pepper. Serve immediately.

BRAISED BEEF WITH RED WINE, TUSCAN-STYLE *SPEZZATINO DI MANZO ALLA TOSCANA*

SERVES 4   PREPARATION TIME: 20 MINUTES   COOKING TIME: 1½–2 HOURS

The depth of flavour of this dish comes from the long cooking time. The addition of a small amount of chilli cuts through and enhances the richness of the sauce and the meat is meltingly tender.

5 tbsp **olive oil**

1kg/2lb 4oz **beef** suitable for braising, cut into 5cm/2in cubes

2 **onions**, cut in half and sliced

2 cloves **garlic**, crushed

1 **red chilli**, deseeded and finely chopped

2 tbsp **tomato purée**

1 litre/1¾ pints/4 cups **beef stock** *(see page 18)*

1 x 400g/14oz tin **chopped tomatoes**

300ml/10fl oz/1¼ cups **red wine**

4 sprigs fresh **rosemary**

6 fresh **sage leaves**, chopped

salt and freshly ground **black pepper**

1 small handful **flat-leaf parsley**, chopped

1 recipe quantity **"wet" polenta** *(see page 27)*, to serve

1 **HEAT** 3 tablespoons of the oil in a large saucepan over a medium heat. Add half the beef and brown lightly on all sides. Set on one side. Repeat with the remaining beef, then set aside with the first batch.

2 **ADD** the remaining oil to the pan and heat through. Toss in the onions, garlic and chilli and cook over a medium heat until the onions are soft and translucent.

3 **STIR** in the tomato purée and cook, still stirring, for 1 minute. Pour over the beef stock, tomatoes and red wine and stir to combine.

4 **RETURN** the meat to the pan. Add the rosemary and sage and season to taste with salt and pepper.

5 **SIMMER** over a low heat, partially covered, for 1½–2 hours until the beef is really tender and the sauce has thickened slightly. Check the seasoning and adjust if necessary. Serve sprinkled with the chopped parsley, accompanied by a helping of "wet" polenta.

MEATBALLS WITH TOMATO SAUCE AND CRUSTY BREAD

POLPETTE AL SUGO

SERVES 4   PREPARATION TIME: 35 MINUTES   COOKING TIME: 45 MINUTES

This delicious mix of lightly spiced meatballs, fresh tomato sauce and melted cheese will leave you using the bread to mop up every last drop of juice.

400g/14oz minced **beef**

400g/14oz minced **veal**

1 **onion**, finely diced

3 tbsp fresh **white breadcrumbs**

1 large handful **flat-leaf parsley**, chopped

leaves from a small handful fresh **rosemary sprigs**, chopped

1 **egg**

salt and freshly ground **black pepper**

2 tbsp **olive oil**

1 recipe quantity **fresh tomato sauce** *(see page 23)*

1 ball **mozzarella cheese**, freshly grated

8 tbsp freshly grated **Parmesan cheese**

1 small handful fresh **basil leaves**, torn

1 loaf crusty **bread**

1 PREHEAT the oven to 180°C/350°F/Gas 4.

2 MIX together the minced beef, minced veal, onion, breadcrumbs, parsley, rosemary and egg in a large bowl. Season to taste with salt and pepper.

3 ROLL the meat mixture into small, bite-size balls and set on one side.

4 HEAT the oil in a large non-stick frying pan over a medium heat. Add half the meatballs and cook until lightly browned all over. Remove from the pan and set aside. Repeat with the remaining meatballs and set aside with the first batch. Transfer all the meatballs to a casserole dish large enough to hold them in one layer.

5 POUR the tomato sauce over the top of the meatballs and sprinkle over the grated mozzarella and Parmesan cheeses. Bake in the hot oven for about 45 minutes, until the cheese is lightly browned and the sauce is bubbling. Stir in the torn basil leaves (or reserve, and scatter over just before serving) and serve immediately, accompanied by the crusty bread.

VEAL SHANKS WITH WHITE WINE

OSSO BUCO ALLA MILANESE

SERVES 4   PREPARATION TIME: 30 MINUTES   COOKING TIME: 2 HOURS

This hearty casserole is ideal for serving up on a frosty winter night.

4 x 3cm/1¼in-thick, centre-cut slices **veal** shin

150g/5½oz **plain flour**, seasoned with **salt** and freshly ground **black pepper**

8 tbsp **olive oil**

25g/1oz **butter**

1 **onion**, diced

1 **carrot**, diced

1 stick **celery**, diced

2 cloves **garlic**, crushed

2 **bay leaves**

3 sprigs fresh **thyme**

250ml/9fl oz/1 cup dry **white wine**

1 x 400g/14oz tin chopped **tomatoes**

250ml/9fl oz/1 cup **beef stock** *(see page 18)*

1 recipe quantity **saffron risotto** *(see page 94)*, to serve

1 PREHEAT the oven to 170°C/325°F/Gas 3

2 ROLL the veal pieces in the seasoned flour until lightly coated and set on one side. Heat 4 tablespoons of the oil in a large sauté pan (see page 17) over a medium heat. Add the veal and brown lightly on all sides. Transfer to a large, ovenproof casserole dish.

3 WIPE the sauté pan clean and add the remaining oil with the butter. Place over a very low heat until the butter has melted. Toss in the onion and cook for 3–4 minutes until soft, but not brown, then add the carrot, celery and garlic and cook for a further 3–4 minutes.

4 STIR in the bay leaves, thyme, white wine, tomatoes and beef stock and season to taste with salt and pepper. Pour over the veal in the casserole dish. Cover the dish tightly with foil.

5 COOK in the hot oven for 1½–2 hours, until the meat is tender and falling off the bone. Serve with a helping of the saffron risotto.

GRILLED STEAK, FLORENTINE-STYLE, WITH STUFFED MUSHROOMS

TAGLIATA CON I FUNGHI

SERVES 4 PREPARATION TIME: 15 MINUTES COOKING TIME: 20 MINUTES

Grilled steak is popular in Florence and is usually so large that it extends over the entire plate. This more elegant version matches the steak with a roasted mushroom, stuffed with a fragrant mix of fennel, garlic, tomato, cheese and basil.

2 tbsp olive oil, plus extra for greasing

8 large field mushrooms

1 small bulb fennel, finely chopped

8 tbsp finely chopped sun-dried tomatoes

1 clove garlic, crushed

75g/2½oz fontina cheese, grated

40g/1½oz Parmesan cheese, grated

1 small handful fresh basil leaves, torn

salt and freshly ground black pepper

4 sirloin steaks, around 200g/7oz each, trimmed

extra-virgin olive oil, to serve

1 GREASE a baking tray with a little olive oil. Remove the stalks from the mushrooms and dice very finely with 4 of the caps, then set on one side. Arrange the 4 remaining mushroom caps, open side up, on the greased tray and also set aside. Preheat the oven to 180°C/350°F/Gas 4.

2 HEAT the remaining oil in a large sauté pan (see page 17) over a low heat. Add the fennel and cook for 5 minutes, until soft. Toss in the sun-dried tomatoes, garlic and diced mushrooms and cook for another 2–3 minutes. Remove from the pan and set aside to cool.

3 BLEND the grated cheeses and basil into the cooled mushroom mixture and season to taste with salt and pepper. Spoon equal amounts of the mixture over the 4 mushroom caps on the baking tray.

4 COOK the stuffed mushrooms in the preheated oven for about 20 minutes, until the mushrooms are tender.

5 SEASON the steaks well with salt and pepper. Heat a griddle pan or grill until really hot and use to cook the steaks to your liking. Serve each with a roasted mushroom, drizzled with extra-virgin olive oil.

PORK FILLETS WITH WHITE WINE AND ROSEMARY

FILETTO DI MAIALE AL VINO BIANCO E ROSMARINO

SERVES 4   PREPARATION TIME: 20 MINUTES   COOKING TIME: 10 MINUTES

This is the perfect recipe for a quick supper. The rosemary in the sauce gives it a delicious uplifting freshness.

2 **pork** fillets, approximately 500g/1lb 2oz each, trimmed

70g/2½oz **plain flour**, seasoned with **salt** and freshly ground **black pepper**

100g/3½oz **butter**

1 tbsp **olive oil**

5 tbsp dry **white wine**

150ml/5fl oz/½ cup **chicken stock** *(see page 18)*

1 handful fresh **rosemary**, chopped

1 CUT each pork fillet, slightly on the diagonal, into six thin slices, or escalopes. Dip these in the seasoned flour to coat them well.

2 HEAT half the butter with the oil in a large sauté pan (see page 17). Add half the pork escalopes and cook for about 2 minutes on each side, until lightly browned. Remove from the pan and keep warm. Repeat with the remaining escalopes, then set aside with the first batch.

3 ADD the white wine, chicken stock and fresh rosemary to the pan and allow to bubble up for 1 minute. Whisk in the remaining butter and season to taste with salt and pepper.

4 RETURN the pork to the pan and leave for 1 minute. Divide between 4 warm serving plates. Serve immediately.

LIVER WITH ONIONS

FEGATO ALLA VENEZIANA

SERVES 4   PREPARATION TIME: 15 MINUTES   COOKING TIME: 20 MINUTES

The sweetness of the onions contrasts brilliantly with the liver.

---

2 tbsp **olive oil**

55g/2oz **butter**

2 large **onions**, very finely sliced

1 clove **garlic**, crushed

500g/1lb 2oz **calves' liver**, membranes removed and sliced thinly

1 large handful **flat-leaf parsley**, chopped

7 tbsp dry **white wine**

salt and freshly ground **black pepper**

1 recipe quantity **"wet" polenta** *(see page 27)*

1 HEAT the olive oil with the butter in a large sauté pan (see page 17). Add the onions and garlic. Stir to coat them well, then turn the heat down to very low and cook, stirring occasionally, for 10–15 minutes, until soft and golden.

2 REMOVE the onions and garlic from the pan and set on one side. Turn the heat up to high. Add the slices of liver and cook for about 1–2 minutes on each side, until golden brown (the inside should remain pink). Return the onions to the pan with the parsley and white wine and cook for a further 2 minutes.

3 SEASON to taste with salt and pepper and divide between 4 warm serving plates. Serve immediately, accompanied by the "wet" polenta.

LEG OF LAMB WITH HERB CRUST

COSCIOTTO D'AGNELLO IN CROSTA D'ERBE

SERVES 4–6   PREPARATION TIME: 10 MINUTES
COOKING TIME: 1–1½ HOURS, PLUS 15 MINUTES RESTING TIME

This recipe is fabulous for a casual lunch or dinner. The crunchy herb topping gives the lamb a really special touch.

1.8–2kg/4–4½lb leg of **lamb**

salt and freshly ground **black pepper**

6 tbsp fresh **white breadcrumbs**

2 tbsp freshly grated **Parmesan cheese**

2 cloves **garlic**, crushed

1 handful fresh **oregano**, finely chopped

1 handful fresh **rosemary**, finely chopped

1 handful **flat-leaf parsley**, finely chopped

3 tbsp **olive oil**

250ml/9fl oz/1 cup **warm water**

1 PREHEAT the oven to 200°C/400°F/Gas 6. Place the lamb in a roasting tin and cut several slashes in the top of the meat using a sharp knife. Season well with salt and pepper.

2 MIX together the breadcrumbs, cheese, garlic, oregano, rosemary, parsley and olive oil in a bowl to make a paste. Spread this mixture over the top of the lamb and rub it well into the cut surface. Pour the warm water into the base of the pan.

3 ROAST the lamb in the hot oven for 15 minutes per 500g/1lb 2oz weight for medium-rare meat, or for 20 minutes for medium.

4 REMOVE the lamb from the oven and leave to rest in a warm place for 15 minutes to allow the juices to settle. Slice and serve.

VEAL ESCALOPES WITH LEMON AND CAPERS

PICCATA DI VITELLO AL LIMONE E CAPPERI

SERVES 4   PREPARATION TIME: 10 MINUTES   COOKING TIME: 15 MINUTES

The slight tanginess that the lemon brings to the sauce complements the veal beautifully.

4 **veal** escalopes (around 125g/4½oz each)

70g/2½oz **plain flour**, seasoned with **salt** and freshly ground **black pepper**

1 tbsp **olive oil**

25g/1oz **butter**

juice and grated rind of 1 **lemon**

175ml/6fl oz dry **white wine**

175ml/6fl oz **chicken** or **vegetable stock** *(see page 18 or 19)*

2 tbsp **capers**, drained and rinsed

2 tbsp **flat-leaf parsley**, chopped

1 PLACE the veal escalopes between 2 pieces of clear film and beat with the rounded end of a rolling pin or the flat side of a meat mallet until really thin. Dip each piece of veal in the seasoned flour until lightly coated.

2 HEAT the oil and butter in a large sauté pan (see page 17). Add the veal and cook for about 2 minutes on each side, until lightly browned. Remove from the pan, set on one side and keep warm.

3 ADD the lemon juice and rind, the white wine and the chicken stock to the pan and bring to the boil. Allow to boil rapidly for 3–4 minutes, until about half the liquid has evaporated. Lower the heat.

4 RETURN the veal to the pan and coat well with the sauce, then stir in the capers and chopped parsley.

5 SEASON to taste with salt and pepper and serve immediately.

VEAL WITH TUNA SAUCE

VITELLO TONNATO

SERVES 4 PREPARATION TIME: 30 MINUTES
COOKING TIME: 1 HOUR, PLUS 2 HOURS COOLING TIME

This recipe makes a great addition to any summer menu. At first glance the mix of flavours may seem a little unusual, but they work together really well.

800g/1lb 12oz boneless **veal** topside

300ml/10½fl oz/1¼ cups dry **white wine**

1 **onion**, quartered

1 small **carrot**, chopped

1 stick **celery**, chopped

2 cloves **garlic**, chopped

2 **bay leaves**

3 **black peppercorns**

2 hard-boiled **egg yolks**

1 x 200g/7oz tin **tuna** in water, well drained

3 **anchovy** fillets, drained and rinsed

1 tbsp **capers**, rinsed, plus extra to garnish

2 tbsp **extra-virgin olive oil**

juice and grated rind of 1 **lemon**, plus slices
    to garnish

freshly ground **black pepper**

1 PLACE the veal in a large saucepan. Add the white wine, onion, carrot, celery, garlic, bay leaves and peppercorns. Add just enough cold water to cover. Bring to the boil, turn down the heat and leave to simmer gently for 1 hour. Turn off the heat and leave the veal to cool in the liquid.

2 COMBINE the egg yolks, tuna, anchovies and capers in a blender or food processor. With the motor running, slowly pour the olive oil in a thin stream into the blender or food processor, until it is absorbed and the mixture is smooth. Transfer to a bowl, stir in the lemon juice and rind and season to taste with pepper.

3 REMOVE the veal from the poaching liquid, slice thinly and arrange on a serving platter. Strain the liquid and add just enough to the tuna sauce to give it the consistency of double cream.

4 POUR the tuna sauce over the sliced veal to coat it. Garnish with the extra capers and lemon slices and serve.

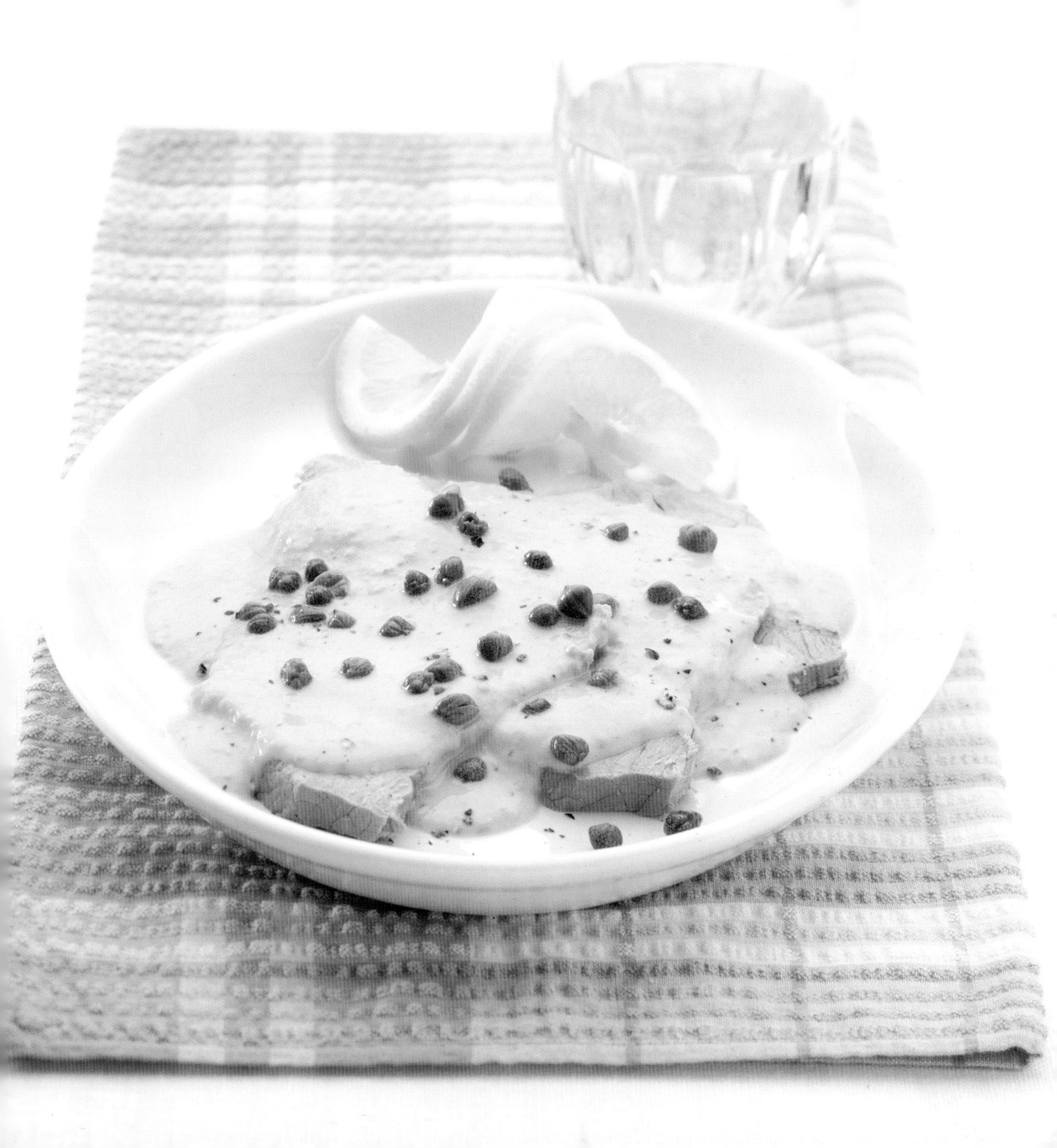

CHICKEN WITH WHITE WINE, TOMATOES AND VEGETABLES *POLLO ALLA CACCIATORA*

SERVES 4   PREPARATION TIME: 35 MINUTES   COOKING TIME: 25 MINUTES

The aroma from this rustic chicken dish, as it bubbles away gently on the stove, is utterly irresistible.

4 **chicken** thighs and 4 drumsticks

4 tbsp **olive oil**

1 large **onion**, sliced

1 **carrot**, finely diced

1 stick **celery**, finely diced

150g/5½oz thickly sliced **pancetta**, finely diced

150g/5½oz button **mushrooms**, sliced

2 cloves **garlic**, crushed

1 tbsp **tomato purée**

1 x 400g/14oz tin **chopped tomatoes**

4 fresh **tomatoes**, peeled, deseeded and chopped

7 tbsp dry **white wine**

3 sprigs fresh **oregano**, chopped

1 **bay leaf**

salt and freshly ground **black pepper**

1 PLACE the chicken in a large bowl and mix with 2 tablespoons of the olive oil until well coated. Heat a large, high-sided sauté pan (see page 17), add half the chicken, and cook over a medium-high heat for about 7–10 minutes until lightly browned on all sides. Remove from the pan with a slotted spoon and set on one side. Repeat with the remaining chicken and set aside with the first batch.

2 WIPE out the pan with kitchen paper. Add the remaining oil and heat over a medium heat. Toss in the onion, carrot and celery and cook for 3 minutes, stirring often to prevent browning. Add the pancetta, mushrooms and garlic and cook for a further 2 minutes.

3 STIR in the tomato purée, tinned tomatoes, fresh tomatoes, white wine, oregano and the bay leaf, and season to taste with salt and pepper.

4 RETURN the chicken to the pan, lower the heat and leave to simmer gently, covered, for 25 minutes, until the chicken is completely cooked through and the sauce has thickened slightly. Serve.

DEVILLED CHICKEN

POLLO ALLA DIAVOLA

SERVES 4   PREPARATION TIME: 35 MINUTES   COOKING TIME: 20 MINUTES

This recipe is traditionally prepared using poussins (small chickens), which are perfect for cooking under a domestic grill. The amount of chilli added to the marinade can be varied, according to how "hot" you like your food.

4 **poussins** (small chickens), around 800g/1lb 12oz each

8 tbsp **olive oil**

juice and rind of 2 large **lemons**

2 small **red chillies**, deseeded and finely diced

2 cloves **garlic**, crushed

2 handfuls **flat-leaf parsley**, finely chopped

2 tbsp **butter**, softened

lemon wedges, to serve

1 REMOVE the backbone from each poussin, using a pair of poultry shears or strong kitchen scissors, then flatten out. Pierce through with skewers if desired, to retain the shape. Place in a shallow casserole dish, large enough to hold all the birds in a single layer.

2 MIX together the olive oil, lemon juice and rind, diced chillies and garlic in a small bowl and pour over the poussins. Leave in the fridge to marinate for about 30 minutes.

3 PREHEAT the grill to high. Place the poussins on a large grill pan and cook under the hot grill for 5–7 minutes, basting occasionally with any remaining marinade, until they are golden brown on top. Turn over and cook for a further 5–7 minutes, until golden brown on the other side. Lower the heat to medium and continue grilling the poussins until they are completely cooked. To test, pierce a thigh with a skewer – the juices should run clear, with no trace at all of any blood.

4 COMBINE the parsley and butter in a small bowl. As soon as the birds are cooked, transfer them to 4 warm serving plates, top with the parsley butter mixture and serve, accompanied by the lemon wedges.

CHICKEN WITH TALEGGIO AND PROSCIUTTO

POLLO AL TALEGGIO E PROSCIUTTO

SERVES **4** PREPARATION TIME: **10** MINUTES COOKING TIME: **15–20** MINUTES

Slice through these delicious morsels of tender chicken to reveal the fragrant basil and creamy, melted cheese in the centre.

4 **chicken** breasts, about 200g/7oz each, skin removed

85g/3oz **Taleggio cheese** *(see page 10)*, cut into small cubes

8 fresh **basil leaves**

freshly ground **black pepper**

8 slices **Parma ham** *(see page 13)*

2 tbsp **olive oil**

1 **CUT** a small "pocket" in each chicken breast, taking care not to cut all the way through the meat. Stuff each "pocket" with a quarter of the Taleggio cheese, then press it firmly closed.

2 **PLACE** 2 basil leaves on top of each piece of chicken, season well with pepper and wrap in the Parma ham, allowing 2 slices for each breast. The ham should be wrapped around the centre of the chicken breast but not encase it completely. Brush each breast lightly with oil. Preheat the oven to 200°C/400°F/Gas 6.

3 **HEAT** a large frying pan over a medium heat. Add the prepared chicken and cook for about 2 minutes on each side, until lightly browned all over. Remove from the frying pan and arrange in a single layer on a baking tray.

4 **BAKE** the chicken in the hot oven for 10–15 minutes, until cooked through. Remove from the oven and leave to rest for about 5 minutes before serving. Serve with oven-baked potatoes, if desired (see page 138).

CHARGRILLED RED MULLET WITH OLIVES AND POTATOES

TRIGLIA GRIGLIATA CON OLIVE E PATATE

SERVES 4   PREPARATION TIME: 20 MINUTES   COOKING TIME: 10 MINUTES

The flavours are superbly matched in this simple, quick-to-prepare dish.

8 **red mullet** fillets, about 100g/3½oz each

2 tbsp **olive oil**

1 small **red onion**, finely sliced

8 tbsp pimento-stuffed **green olives**

juice and grated rind of 1 **lemon**

150g/5½oz marinated **artichoke hearts**, cut into small chunks

4 tbsp **flat-leaf parsley**, roughly chopped

5 tbsp **extra-virgin olive oil**

500g/1lb 2oz baby **new potatoes**, cut in half

freshly ground **black pepper**

lemon wedges, to serve

1 BRUSH the red mullet lightly with the olive oil and leave in the fridge while preparing the rest of the ingredients.

2 MIX together the red onion, green olives, lemon juice and rind, artichoke hearts, parsley and 3 tablespoons of the extra-virgin olive oil in a large bowl and set on one side. Boil or steam the potatoes until tender. Add the warm potatoes to the onion, olive and artichoke mixture, season to taste with pepper and combine well. Set on one side and keep warm.

3 HEAT a griddle pan (see page 16) or large frying pan until hot. Remove the fish from the fridge and place in the hot pan. Cook for about 2 minutes on each side, until cooked through.

4 DIVIDE the warm potato mixture between 4 warm serving plates. Top each serving with 2 of the freshly cooked fish fillets, drizzle over the remaining extra-virgin olive oil and serve with the lemon wedges.

SEAFOOD WITH TOMATO

CACCIUCCO ALLA LIVORNESE

SERVES 4 PREPARATION TIME: 20 MINUTES COOKING TIME: 55 MINUTES

*Traditionally this recipe was prepared using five different types
of seafood – one for every "c" in the word "cacciucco".*

3 tbsp **olive oil**

1 **onion**, finely chopped

2 cloves **garlic**, crushed

1 **carrot**, diced

1 stick **celery**, diced

2 tbsp **tomato purée**

1 x 400g/14oz tin **chopped tomatoes**

100ml/3½fl oz/1 glass dry **white wine**

500ml/17fl oz/2 cups **fish stock** *(see page 19)*

1 handful fresh **dill**, roughly chopped

500g/1lb 2oz **monkfish** fillets

12 fresh **mussels**

150g/5½oz shelled **scallops**

150g/5½oz raw **prawns**, shelled

salt and freshly ground **black pepper**

1 handful **flat-leaf parsley**, chopped

1 HEAT the oil in a large sauté pan (see page 17). Add the onion and cook for 2–3 minutes, until just soft. Add the garlic, carrot and celery and cook for another 3 minutes.

2 STIR in the tomato purée and cook for 2 minutes, then add the chopped tomatoes, white wine, fish stock and dill. Lower the heat, and leave to simmer gently for 30–40 minutes, until the vegetables are tender and the sauce has reduced by about one-third and thickened slightly.

3 CUT the monkfish into bite-sized pieces. Clean the mussels thoroughly and remove the beards with a sharp knife. Discard any shells that are broken or remain open when tapped.

4 ADD the monkfish to the hot tomato sauce and cook for 5 minutes. Toss in the mussels, scallops and prawns and cook for a further 4 minutes or until all of the fish is cooked through.

5 SEASON to taste with salt and pepper, sprinkle over the chopped parsley and serve immediately.

MARINATED SWORDFISH

PESCE SPADA MARINATO

SERVES 4 PREPARATION TIME: 35 MINUTES COOKING TIME: 8 MINUTES

*The subtle addition of chilli and lemon helps to lift the rich flavour
of the swordfish.*

4 swordfish steaks, about 200g/7oz each

juice and grated rind of 2 lemons

4 tbsp olive oil

1 small red chilli, deseeded and finely diced

1 clove garlic, crushed

7 tbsp dry white wine

freshly ground black pepper

extra-virgin olive oil, to serve

1 handful flat-leaf parsley, roughly chopped

1 ARRANGE the swordfish steaks in a shallow ovenproof dish, large enough to hold them in a single layer. Mix together the lemon juice and rind, olive oil, chilli, garlic and white wine in a small bowl and pour over the fish. Leave to marinate in the fridge for 30 minutes.

2 HEAT a large frying pan over a medium-high heat. Add the fish steaks, with any marinade, and cook for about 3 minutes on each side, until lightly browned and cooked through. Season to taste with pepper.

3 DIVIDE the fish steaks between 4 warm serving plates. Drizzle over a little extra-virgin olive oil, sprinkle with the chopped parsley and serve.

SEA BASS WITH SALSA VERDE

BRANZINO CON SALSA VERDE

SERVES 4   PREPARATION TIME: 15 MINUTES, PLUS 2 HOURS CHILLING TIME
COOKING TIME: 10 MINUTES

The salsa verde is at its best when made a few hours in advance and kept in the fridge until needed. It goes as well with chicken as it does with fish.

8 tbsp fresh **white breadcrumbs**

1 tbsp **milk**

2 **anchovy** fillets, rinsed

1 tbsp **capers**, rinsed

1 large handful each **flat-leaf parsley**, **mint** and **basil**, finely chopped

1 clove **garlic**, crushed

4 tbsp **extra-virgin olive oil**

juice of ½ **lemon**

salt and freshly ground **black pepper**

8 **sea bass** fillets, about 100g/3½oz each

1 tbsp **olive oil**

1 MIX together the breadcrumbs and milk in a bowl. Chop the anchovy fillets and capers together very finely and add to the breadcrumb mixture. Stir in the finely chopped herbs, garlic, extra-virgin olive oil and lemon juice, then season to taste with salt and pepper. Leave this salsa verde mixture in the fridge for at least 2 hours, preferably longer, before using.

2 TRIM the fish fillets, taking care to remove any remaining bones.

3 HEAT the tablespoon of olive oil in a large frying pan. Add the sea bass fillets and cook for about 2 minutes on each side, until just cooked. Divide the fish between 4 warm serving plates and serve immediately, with a large spoonful of the salsa verde on top of each serving.

SOLE VENETIAN-STYLE

SOGLIOLA ALLA VENEZIANA

SERVES 4   PREPARATION TIME: 15 MINUTES   COOKING TIME: 15 MINUTES

The fresh herbs blend beautifully with the delicate flavour of the sole.

70g/2½oz **butter**

1 **onion**, diced

1 clove **garlic**, crushed

8 tbsp fresh **white breadcrumbs**

1 large handful **flat-leaf parsley**, chopped

1 large handful fresh **mint**, chopped

1 tbsp **olive oil**

4 whole **lemon** or **Dover sole**, approximately 300g/10½oz each, gutted and trimmed

salt and freshly ground **black pepper**

juice of 1 **lemon**

1 MELT the butter in a saucepan over a low heat. Add the onion and garlic and cook for about 2–3 minutes, until the onion begins to soften.

2 STIR in the breadcrumbs, parsley and mint and mix well. Set on one side to cool. Preheat the oven to 180°C/350°F/Gas 4.

3 OIL a rimmed baking tray, large enough to hold the fish in a single layer, with a splash of the olive oil. Arrange the fish on the tray, drizzle over the remaining oil, then spread the herbed breadcrumbs equally over the fish. Season to taste with salt and pepper and drizzle over the lemon juice.

4 BAKE in the hot oven for about 15 minutes, until the fish is cooked through and the breadcrumbs are golden brown. Serve immediately.

GRILLED TUNA WITH RED PEPPER SAUCE

TONNO ALLA GRIGLIA CON PEPERONATA

SERVES 4   PREPARATION TIME: 10 MINUTES   COOKING TIME: 25 MINUTES

The colours in the red pepper sauce are as spectacular as the taste.

---

4 **tuna** steaks, approximately 200g/7oz each

4 tbsp **olive oil**

1 **onion**, chopped

1 **red chilli**, deseeded and finely chopped

2 cloves **garlic**, crushed

3 **red peppers**, finely sliced

3 large ripe **tomatoes**, peeled, deseeded and chopped

salt and freshly ground **black pepper**

1 BRUSH the tuna steaks lightly with a little of the olive oil and leave in the fridge while preparing the pepper sauce.

2 HEAT the remaining oil in a large sauté pan (see page 17), add the onion and cook for 2–3 minutes, until soft. Add the chilli and garlic and cook a further 1 minute. Stir in the peppers and tomatoes and leave to simmer for 10–15 minutes, until the peppers are soft and the sauce has thickened. Season to taste with salt and pepper, then set aside and keep warm.

3 HEAT a large griddle pan (see page 16) or frying pan over a medium-high heat. Remove the tuna steaks from the fridge and place in the pan. Cook for about 2 minutes on each side, so that the tuna is browned on the outside, but still slightly pink in the centre.

4 TRANSFER the tuna steaks to 4 warm serving plates. Spoon over the red pepper and serve immediately.

OVEN-BAKED POTATOES

PATATE AL FORNO

SERVES 4   PREPARATION TIME: 15 MINUTES   COOKING TIME: 50 MINUTES

The lemon gives these delicious golden potatoes a refreshing zing.

600g/1lb 5oz **potatoes**, peeled and cut into approximately 1cm/½in cubes

3 cloves **garlic**, crushed

juice of 1 **lemon**

3 tbsp **olive oil**

1 large handful fresh **rosemary**, roughly chopped

salt and freshly ground **black pepper**

1 PREHEAT the oven to 200°C/400°F/Gas 6.

2 PLACE all of the ingredients in a large bowl, seasoning well with salt and pepper, and toss to combine.

3 SPREAD over a large, lightly greased baking tray and cook in the hot oven for 45–50 minutes, until the potatoes are golden brown and cooked through. Turn the potatoes 2 or 3 times during cooking, so that they brown evenly.

4 TIP the potatoes into a warm serving dish and serve.

AUBERGINE GRATIN

MELANZANE GRATINATE

SERVES 4   PREPARATION TIME: 20 MINUTES   COOKING TIME: 30 MINUTES

This gratin makes a delicious and satisfying supper dish and also makes a good accompaniment to simple meat and poultry dishes.

2 large **aubergines**, cut into cubes

3 **courgettes**, cut into cubes

1 **onion**, diced

1 clove **garlic**, crushed

1 small handful fresh **thyme**, roughly chopped

4 tbsp **olive oil**

salt and freshly ground **black pepper**

3 tbsp freshly grated **Parmesan cheese**

8 tbsp grated **mozzarella cheese**

1 PREHEAT the oven to 180°C/350°F/Gas 4. Place the cubes of aubergine and courgette with the onion, garlic and fresh thyme in an ovenproof casserole dish. Add the olive oil and stir to mix well. Season to taste with salt and pepper.

2 COVER the dish with foil or a well-fitting lid and cook in the hot oven for 15–20 minutes, until the vegetables are beginning to soften.

3 UNCOVER the dish and sprinkle the Parmesan and mozzarella cheeses over the top. Return to the oven for a further 10 minutes, until the vegetables are soft and the cheese topping is golden brown. Serve.

POTATO AND HERB GRATIN

PATATE GRATINATE ALLE ERBE AROMATICHE

SERVES 4   PREPARATION TIME: 20 MINUTES   COOKING TIME: 50 MINUTES

Make this for a Sunday lunch or a special dinner. It goes together perfectly with grilled and roasted meats, especially roast lamb.

800g/1lb 12oz **potatoes**, thinly sliced

2 sprigs each fresh **thyme**, **sage** and **rosemary**

500ml/17fl oz/2 cups **double cream**

100g/3½oz **butter**

1 clove **garlic**, crushed

salt and freshly ground **black pepper**

4 tbsp freshly grated **Parmesan cheese**

1 PREHEAT the oven to 200°C/400°F/Gas 6.

2 LAYER the potato slices in a large ovenproof dish.

3 HEAT the cream, butter, garlic and herbs in a medium saucepan over a low heat until the mixture just begins to simmer. Remove from the heat and leave to stand for 10 minutes for the flavours to infuse. Season to taste with salt and pepper.

4 STRAIN the cream mixture over the potatoes, discarding the herbs and garlic. Sprinkle over the Parmesan cheese and bake in the hot oven for 30–35 minutes, until the potatoes are soft and the top is golden brown. Allow to cool slightly, then serve.

WARM CANNELLINI BEANS WITH TOMATOES AND HERBS *FAGIOLI ALL'UCCELLETTO*

SERVES 4   PREPARATION TIME: 10 MINUTES, PLUS 8 HOURS SOAKING TIME
COOKING TIME: 1–1½ HOURS

The fresh herbs and splash of balsamic vinegar provide a touch of sharpness that contrasts well with the creaminess of the warm beans.

200g/7oz dried **cannellini beans**

1 **bay leaf**

3 sprigs fresh **rosemary**

3 sprigs fresh **thyme**

4 tbsp **extra-virgin olive oil**

1 **red onion**, sliced

1 clove **garlic**, crushed

3 **tomatoes**, peeled, deseeded and chopped

1 large handful **flat-leaf parsley**, chopped

1 large handful fresh **rosemary**, chopped

2 tbsp **balsamic vinegar** *(see page 10)*

salt and freshly ground **black pepper**

1 SOAK the dried beans in a pan of cold water for at least 8 hours, preferably overnight. Drain, place in a large clean saucepan and cover with plenty of fresh cold water. Add the bay leaf, rosemary and thyme and bring to the boil. Lower the heat and leave to simmer gently for about 1 hour, until the beans are just soft. Drain, rinse thoroughly in fresh cold water and set on one side.

2 HEAT the oil in a large sauté pan (see page 17). Add the red onion and cook over a low heat for about 3 minutes, until soft. Add the garlic and cook for a further 1 minute.

3 STIR in the tomatoes and cooked beans. Turn the heat up to medium and leave to simmer for 5 minutes.

4 MIX in the chopped parsley and rosemary, then add the balsamic vinegar and season to taste with salt and pepper. Remove from the heat and leave to cool slightly. Serve warm.

PEAS WITH PANCETTA AND MINT

PISELLI CON PANCETTA E MENTA

SERVES 4   PREPARATION TIME: 10 MINUTES   COOKING TIME: 25 MINUTES

With the tang of fresh green mint and the salty sharpness of the pinky-brown pancetta, this is a dish that looks and tastes fabulous.

500g/1lb 2oz shelled fresh **peas**

1 tbsp **olive oil**

100g/3½oz thickly sliced **pancetta**, diced

1 handful fresh **mint**, finely chopped

25g/1oz **butter**

freshly ground **black pepper**

1 BRING a large pan of salted water to the boil. Add the peas and return to the boil. Lower the heat slightly and leave to simmer for about 15 minutes, until the peas are tender. Drain and set aside.

2 HEAT the oil in a sauté pan (see page 17). Add the pancetta and cook for about 3–4 minutes, until just starting to brown.

3 TOSS in the cooked peas, followed by the chopped mint and butter, then season to taste with pepper. Remove from the heat, stir well to combine and serve.

CHICKPEA SALAD WITH TUNA

INSALATA DI CECI E TONNO

SERVES 4 PREPARATION TIME: 10 MINUTES, PLUS 30 MINUTES STANDING TIME

This quickly prepared salad is brimming with fresh flavours. Serve it up for lunch with chunks of crusty bread or as a side dish at a dinner or party.

2 x 410g/14½oz tins **chickpeas**, rinsed and drained

2 x 185g/6½oz tins **tuna** in brine, rinsed, drained and flaked

1 clove **garlic**, crushed

1 **red onion**, finely sliced

juice of 2 **lemons**

7 tbsp **extra-virgin olive oil**

freshly ground **black pepper**

2 handfuls **flat-leaf parsley**, chopped

1 handful **rocket**

1 COMBINE the chickpeas, tuna, garlic and red onion in a large bowl and set on one side.

2 WHISK together the lemon juice and olive oil in a small bowl or jug and pour over the chickpea mixture.

3 SEASON well with pepper, cover and leave to stand in a cool place for 30 minutes to allow the flavours to blend. Mix in the chopped parsley.

4 PLACE the rocket on a serving platter, spoon over the chickpea and tuna mixture and serve.

FRESH TOMATO SALAD WITH COUNTRY BREAD *PANZANELLA*

SERVES 4   PREPARATION TIME: 5 MINUTES, PLUS 30 MINUTES STANDING TIME

This stunning combination of chewy bread, fresh tomatoes and tangy red-wine vinegar makes a refreshing addition to any summer meal.

200g/7oz loaf **ciabatta bread**, crusts removed and cut into small cubes

3 large fresh **tomatoes**, cut into small chunks

1 **yellow pepper**, cut into small chunks

½ **cucumber**, peeled and cut into small chunks

2 **spring onions**, thinly sliced

1 small handful fresh **basil leaves**, torn

7 tbsp **extra-virgin olive oil**

3 tbsp **red-wine vinegar**

1 clove **garlic**, crushed

1 PLACE the bread cubes with the chunks of tomato, yellow pepper and cucumber in a large serving bowl. Add the spring onions and basil and mix well together. Leave to stand in a cool place for 30 minutes to allow the flavours to blend.

2 WHISK together the extra-virgin olive oil, red-wine vinegar and garlic in a small bowl or jug. Pour over the bread, tomato, pepper and cucumber salad mixture, toss to mix in and serve immediately.

TOMATO, MINT AND RED ONION SALAD

INSALATA DI POMODORO, MENTA E CIPOLLA

SERVES 4   PREPARATION TIME: 15 MINUTES

Mint serves as an uplifting and surprising contrast to the tangy tomato and crisp red onion in this salad.

4 large fresh **tomatoes**, finely sliced

½ small **red onion**, finely sliced

1 small handful fresh **mint**, chopped

3½ tbsp **extra-virgin olive oil**

juice and grated rind of 1 **lemon**

freshly ground **black pepper**

1 ARRANGE the tomato slices on a serving plate, slightly overlapping. Sprinkle over the red onion and the mint.

2 MIX together the extra-virgin olive oil and the lemon juice and rind in a small bowl or jug and drizzle over the tomato and onion salad.

3 SEASON to taste with pepper and serve immediately.

FRESH MOZZARELLA AND TOMATO SALAD

INSALATA CAPRESE

SERVES 4   PREPARATION TIME: 15 MINUTES

The key to the success of this simple dish lies in the freshness and quality of the ingredients. Use only the very best available.

500g/1lb 2oz **buffalo mozzarella**

3 large, ripe, fresh **tomatoes**

1 small handful fresh **basil leaves**

salt and freshly ground **black pepper**

4 tbsp **extra-virgin olive oil**

2 tbsp **white-wine vinegar**

1 tbsp **capers**, rinsed

1 SLICE the mozzarella and tomatoes thinly and arrange on a serving platter. Scatter over the basil leaves and season to taste with salt and a generous grinding of pepper.

2 WHISK together the extra-virgin olive oil and white-wine vinegar in a small bowl or jug, then drizzle over the tomatoes and mozzarella. Scatter the capers over the top and serve.

ORANGE AND FENNEL SALAD

INSALATA SICILIANA

SERVES 4   PREPARATION TIME: 15 MINUTES

You can make this tangy salad in advance, if you like, but it is best to add the pine nuts just before serving.

4 large **oranges**, peeled and segmented

1 bulb **fennel**, trimmed and finely sliced

1 small handful fresh **dill**, chopped

3 tbsp **extra-virgin olive oil**

1 tbsp **white-wine vinegar**

3 tbsp **pine nuts**, toasted

1 PLACE the oranges, fennel and dill in a large serving bowl.

2 POUR over the olive oil and white-wine vinegar and toss well to combine. Set aside in a cool place, if you wish, until ready to serve.

3 SPRINKLE over the pine nuts and serve immediately.

POTATO SALAD WITH CAPERS

INSALATA DI PATATE CON CAPPERI

SERVES 4 PREPARATION TIME: 10 MINUTES, PLUS 30 MINUTES STANDING TIME
COOKING TIME: 15 MINUTES

Light and fresh, yet satisfying, this will become a warm-weather staple.

750g/1lb 10oz baby **new potatoes**

2 tbsp **capers**, rinsed

3 **spring onions**, finely chopped

2 tbsp **red-wine vinegar**

3½ tbsp **extra-virgin olive oil**

freshly ground **black pepper**

1 BOIL or steam the potatoes in their skins until tender, then set aside to cool. Cut any larger potatoes in quarters or halves, but leave the small ones whole.

2 MIX together all of the ingredients, including the prepared potatoes, in a large serving bowl, seasoning well with pepper.

3 LEAVE to stand for at least 30 minutes before serving to allow the flavours to mix together.

ASPARAGUS SALAD

INSALATA DI ASPARAGI

This sumptuous mix of jewel-like cherry tomatoes and spears of fresh green asparagus creates a feast for the eyes as well as the palate.

750g/1lb 10oz fresh **asparagus**, trimmed

100g/3½oz **cherry tomatoes**, halved

1 small handful fresh **basil leaves**, torn

3 tbsp **extra-virgin olive oil**

1 tbsp **balsamic vinegar** *(see page 10)*

salt and freshly ground **black pepper**

1 STEAM the asparagus for 4–6 minutes, until just tender. Cool immediately under cold running water, pat dry and arrange on a serving platter.

2 MIX together the cherry tomatoes and basil in a bowl and set aside.

3 WHISK together the extra-virgin olive oil and balsamic vinegar in another bowl or jug and season to taste with salt and pepper. Pour over the tomatoes and basil and toss to mix in well.

4 TIP the tomato mixture over the platter of asparagus and serve.

ITALIAN CREAMS

PANNA COTTA

SERVES 4   PREPARATION TIME: 20 MINUTES, PLUS 4 HOURS CHILLING TIME

The Italian name of this traditional dessert translates as "cooked cream". It is very simple to make and tastes delicious served with fresh fruit.

2 sheets **leaf gelatine** *(see page 11)*

200ml/7fl oz/¾ cup **double cream**

200ml/7fl oz/¾ cup **milk**

25g/1oz **caster sugar**

1 tsp **vanilla extract**

fresh **fruit** in season, to serve

icing sugar, to serve

1 PLACE the sheets of gelatine in a large bowl and cover completely with cold water. Leave for 5 minutes, until the gelatine has softened.

2 COMBINE the cream, milk, caster sugar and vanilla extract in a small saucepan. Place over a low heat until just warm. Remove from the heat and set on one side.

3 REMOVE the gelatine from the water and squeeze out any excess moisture. Stir into the warm milk mixture until it dissolves. Leave to cool for about 5–10 minutes.

4 DIVIDE the mixture equally between 4 small ramekins or small glasses and place in the fridge to chill and set for at least 4 hours, preferably overnight. Carefully turn out of the ramekins or glasses, dust with icing sugar, if desired, and serve with a mixture of seasonal fresh fruit.

ZABAGLIONE

SERVES 4   PREPARATION TIME: 5 MINUTES   COOKING TIME: 7 MINUTES

Marsala is a fortified wine that originates in Sicily. It is traditionally used in this luscious, rich and creamy dessert – the perfect ending to any really special meal.

8 **egg yolks**

4 tbsp **caster sugar**

7 tbsp **Marsala wine** *(see page 12)*

8 **sponge-finger biscuits**

1 WHISK together the yolks, sugar and Marsala in a heatproof bowl.

2 PLACE the bowl over a pan of gently simmering water, so that the base of the pan does not touch the water, and continue to whisk vigorously until the mixture is frothy and is just starting to thicken. This should take about 5–7 minutes. Remove the bowl from the heat.

3 POUR the warm egg and Marsala mixture into tall serving glasses and serve immediately, accompanied by the sponge-finger biscuits.

STRAWBERRIES IN BALSAMIC VINEGAR

FRAGOLE CON ACETO BALSAMICO

SERVES 4   PREPARATION TIME: 10 MINUTES

The addition of the balsamic vinegar may seem odd, but it really does help to bring out the full flavour of the fresh strawberries.

300g/10½oz fresh **strawberries**

1 tbsp **caster sugar**

1 tbsp **balsamic vinegar** *(see page 10)*

4 scoops **vanilla ice cream**, to serve

1 WASH and hull the strawberries, cut in half and place in a bowl.

2 SPRINKLE over the sugar and balsamic vinegar and toss well to combine.

3 PLACE a scoop of ice cream on each serving dish and spoon over the strawberries. Serve immediately.

"PICK-ME-UP" TRIFLE

TIRAMISÙ

SERVES 4—6   PREPARATION TIME: 20 MINUTES, PLUS 2 HOURS CHILLING TIME

This sensational combination of fresh coffee, Marsala wine and rich, creamy mascarpone cheese is utterly irresistible.

---

5 **egg yolks**

100g/3½oz **caster sugar**

250g/9oz **mascarpone cheese** *(see page 10)*

2 **egg whites**

350ml/12fl oz/1½ cups **espresso** or strong **coffee**, cold

4 tbsp **Marsala wine**

20 **sponge-finger biscuits**

2 tbsp **cocoa powder**

4 tbsp grated **plain chocolate**

1 WHISK the egg yolks and sugar together in a large bowl, preferably using an electric hand-held whisk, until thick and light in colour. Add the mascarpone and combine well. Set on one side.

2 BEAT the egg whites in a clean bowl until they form stiff peaks, then carefully fold through the mascarpone mixture, using a large metal spoon. Set on one side.

3 MIX together the cold coffee and Marsala wine in another bowl. Dip half the sponge-finger biscuits into the mixture, being sure to soak them well, and use to line the base of a serving dish, approximately 28 x 18cm/11 x 7in. Pour over half of the prepared mascarpone mixture.

4 REPEAT with the remaining biscuits and mascarpone mixture.

5 SPRINKLE the cocoa powder over the top using a sieve, then scatter with the grated chocolate. Refrigerate for at least 2 hours, preferably overnight. Serve.

BAKED PEACHES STUFFED WITH AMARETTI BISCUITS

PESCHE RIPIENE

SERVES 4   PREPARATION TIME: 10 MINUTES   COOKING TIME: 15–20 MINUTES

These delicious peaches, served warm with their amaretti filling, create a spectacular fusion of colour and flavour.

4 ripe yellow **peaches**

100g/3½oz **amaretti biscuits**, crushed

60g/2¼oz **butter**, melted

1 large **egg yolk**

1 tsp freshly grated **nutmeg**

whipped **cream**, to serve

1 PREHEAT the oven to 200°C/400°F/Gas 6.

2 BRUSH an ovenproof dish, large enough to contain the stuffed peaches in a single layer, with a little of the melted butter.

3 CRUSH the amaretti biscuits in a food processor or blender, then mix in the remaining melted butter, egg yolk and nutmeg.

4 HALVE the peaches and remove the stones. Spoon the prepared amaretti filling into each peach cavity and press down firmly. Arrange the stuffed peaches in the prepared ovenproof dish.

5 BAKE in the hot oven for 15–20 minutes until soft and lightly browned. Serve warm with whipped fresh cream.

ICE CREAM WITH ESPRESSO AND FRANGELICO *AFFOGATO AL CAFFÈ*

SERVES 4   PREPARATION TIME: 5 MINUTES

Frangelico is a sweet, hazelnut liqueur from the Liguria region of Italy.
It is particularly good with the hot and cold taste sensations of this dessert.

---

8 scoops **vanilla ice cream**

4 tbsp **espresso coffee**, hot

4 tbsp **Frangelico** liqueur

1 PLACE 2 scoops of ice cream into each of 4 tall serving glasses. Set aside in the freezer until ready to serve.

2 POUR 1 tablespoon of hot espresso coffee and 1 tablespoon of Frangelico liqueur over each glass of ice cream and serve immediately.

LEMON ICE CREAM

GELATO AL LIMONE

SERVES 4 PREPARATION TIME: 20 MINUTES, PLUS FREEZING TIME

Creamy and luscious, this ice cream makes a glorious finale to a meal.

200ml/7fl oz/¾ cup **milk**

4 **egg yolks**

200g/7oz **caster sugar**

juice and grated rind of 2 **lemons**

200ml/7fl oz/¾ cup **double cream**

1 HEAT the milk in a saucepan, over a low heat, until just warm. Set on one side.

2 WHISK together the egg yolks and sugar in a large bowl, then pour in the warm milk, whisking constantly. Return the mixture to the saucepan and stir over a low heat, with a wooden spoon, until the mixture is just thick enough to coat the back of the spoon. Do not allow to boil. Pour into a clean bowl and leave to cool completely.

3 STIR the lemon juice and rind into the cooled mixture, followed by the double cream. Pour into an ice-cream machine and freeze according to the manufacturer's instructions. Serve.

COFFEE ICE CREAM

GELATO AL CAFFÈ

SERVES 4–6   PREPARATION TIME: 20 MINUTES, PLUS FREEZING TIME

Use the best quality coffee for the richest, smoothest flavour.

200ml/7fl oz/¾ cup **milk**

1 **vanilla pod**, split

2 **eggs**

150g/5oz **caster sugar**

175ml/6fl oz/⅔ cup **espresso coffee**, cold

200ml/7fl oz/¾ cup **double cream**

1 HEAT the milk in a saucepan, with the vanilla pod, over a low heat, until just warm. Leave to stand for 5 minutes, then remove the vanilla pod. Scrape out the vanilla seeds with a knife and add them to the milk, discarding the empty pod.

2 WHISK together the eggs and sugar in a large bowl, then pour in the warm milk, whisking constantly. Return the mixture to the saucepan and cook, over a low heat, stirring constantly with a wooden spoon, until the mixture is just thick enough to coat the back of the spoon. Do not allow to boil.

3 POUR into a clean bowl and stir in the espresso coffee. Leave to cool completely.

4 STIR in the cream, then transfer to an ice-cream machine and freeze according to the manufacturer's instructions. Serve.

LEMON RICOTTA CAKE

TORTA DI RICOTTA AL LIMONE

SERVES 6—8   PREPARATION TIME: 30 MINUTES   COOKING TIME: 45 MINUTES

This is a cross between a pudding and a cake. When served warm, the luscious creamy centre is beautifully balanced by the tang of the lemon.

1 tbsp melted **butter**

175g/6oz ground **almonds**

55g/2oz **plain flour**

150g/5½oz **butter**, softened

200g/7oz **caster sugar**

4 **eggs**, separated

200g/7oz **ricotta cheese**

juice and grated rind of 3 **lemons**

icing sugar, to serve

1 PREHEAT the oven to 170°C/325°F/Gas 3. Grease a 20cm/8in, loose-bottomed cake tin with the melted butter. Line the base with baking parchment.

2 MIX together the almonds and flour in a bowl and set on one side.

3 BEAT the butter and sugar together, until light and creamy. Add the egg yolks and continue beating until well combined. Mix in the ricotta cheese, followed by the lemon juice and rind. Fold in the almond and flour mixture until just combined. Set on one side.

4 BEAT the egg whites in a clean bowl until they just start to form stiff peaks, then gently fold into the cake mixture, using a metal spoon.

5 POUR into the prepared cake tin, smooth over the top and bake in the hot oven for about 45 minutes, until lightly browned and still slightly soft in the centre. Allow to cool slightly in the tin, then turn out. Serve warm or at room temperature, dusted with icing sugar.

CHOCOLATE ICE-CREAM SLICE
SEMIFREDDO AL CIOCCOLATO

SERVES 6   PREPARATION TIME: 20 MINUTES, PLUS 4 HOURS FREEZING TIME

This ice-cream style of dessert does not require any churning, so can be frozen by simply popping it into the freezer. It has a rich and powerful chocolate flavour.

500ml/17fl oz/2 cups **double cream**

4 **eggs**, separated

250g/9oz **caster sugar**

12 tbsp **cocoa powder**

2 tbsp **Frangelico** liqueur *(see page 173)*

4 tbsp toasted, chopped **hazelnuts**

fresh **raspberries**, to serve

1 MIX half the cream with the egg yolks, caster sugar and cocoa powder in a saucepan until well combined. Place over a low heat and stir constantly until the mixture thickens and is just starting to boil. Remove from the heat, stir in the Frangelico liqueur and transfer to a large bowl. Leave to cool completely.

2 LINE the base of a 20cm/8in springform cake tin with clear film.

3 WHIP the remaining cream until thick in a clean bowl, then fold into the cold custard mixture. Beat the egg whites until they just start to form stiff peaks, then fold through the cream and custard mixture, using a metal spoon. Pour into the prepared tin and cover with clear film to seal completely. Freeze for at least 4 hours, preferably overnight.

4 REMOVE from the freezer and place in the fridge for about 20 minutes before serving, to soften slightly. Cut into slices and serve, sprinkled with the hazelnuts and a helping of fresh raspberries.

PANFORTE

MAKES ABOUT 24 SLICES   PREPARATION TIME: 25 MINUTES
COOKING TIME: 15 MINUTES, PLUS OVERNIGHT COOLING TIME

This traditional treat from Siena is perfect for rounding off a celebratory dinner in style, especially when served with a glass of chilled vin santo.

175g/6oz each **hazelnuts**, **almonds** and **walnuts**, roasted and roughly chopped

175g/6oz each dried **figs**, dried **apricots** and dried **prunes**, roughly chopped

125g/4½oz **plain flour**

pinch of **white pepper**

1 tsp grated **nutmeg**

½ tsp ground **cloves**

½ tsp ground **coriander**

½ tsp ground **cinnamon**

150g/5½oz **caster sugar**

10 tbsp clear **honey**

icing sugar, to serve

1 LINE a 25cm/10in springform cake tin with baking parchment. Set aside. Preheat the oven to 180°C/350°F/Gas 4.

2 COMBINE the chopped nuts and dried fruit in a large bowl. Add the flour, pepper, nutmeg, cloves, coriander and cinnamon and mix in thoroughly. Set aside.

3 PLACE the sugar and honey in a saucepan and bring to the boil over a low heat, stirring constantly. Allow to boil for 1 minute, then remove from the heat and pour over the fruit and nut mixture, stirring to combine thoroughly. The mixture should be very thick.

4 SPOON into the prepared cake tin and smooth out evenly with slightly wet hands. Bake in the hot oven for 15 minutes. Remove from the oven and leave to cool a little. While still warm, run a sharp knife around the edge to release it from the tin. Leave in the tin to cool completely overnight.

5 REMOVE from the tin and cut into thin slices. Dust lightly with icing sugar just before serving.

WHITE PEACHES WITH RASPBERRIES, MINT AND PROSECCO

PESCE BIANCHE CON LAMPONI, MENTA E PROSECCO

SERVES 4   PREPARATION TIME: 15 MINUTES   COOKING TIME: 5 MINUTES

Prosecco is an Italian white wine, made in the Champagne style, that is light and deliciously fragrant. The combination of luscious white peaches and raspberries, mixed with mint and Prosecco, is simply heaven on earth and just perfect for a warm summer's evening.

125g/4½oz **caster sugar**

170ml/5½fl oz/⅔ cup cold **water**

4 **white peaches**

200g/7oz **raspberries**

1 small handful fresh **mint**, finely shredded

170ml/5½fl oz/⅔ cup dry **Prosecco**, chilled

1 PLACE the sugar and water in a saucepan over a low heat. Stir continuously until the sugar has dissolved completely. Remove from the heat and leave to cool, then set aside in the fridge to chill.

2 SLICE the peaches into a large bowl, then add the raspberries and mint. This should be done no more than 30 minutes before serving – any longer and the peaches will start to brown.

3 MIX together the chilled sugar syrup and Prosecco in a clean jug or bowl and pour over the peaches.

4 SPOON into 4 serving dishes and serve.

PART 3

THE MENUS

*Putting together a **successful** menu is one of the most challenging aspects of **entertaining** and can be a juggling act for even the most accomplished cook. Each of the **suggestions** that follows has been developed with a specific occasion in mind and is organized so that not only are the **flavours**, textures and colours in the various dishes **balanced**, but the amount of preparation and last-minute **touches** that are required are too.*

*Each menu comes with a detailed time-plan, **clearly** explaining exactly when to execute the various stages of the recipes involved. Preparation **notes** giving details of useful **techniques** are also included to make life as easy as possible.*

*While each of the menus has been designed with a particular **occasion** in mind, you should feel **free** to mix and match recipes to suit your own needs. Refer to the time-plans for **guidance**, but do not feel constrained by any of the suggestions. Your cooking should reflect who you are and your **lifestyle** and most importantly be a source of **pleasure** to all who gather around your table.*

SIMPLE LUNCH

TIME PLAN

This is a truly simple lunch to prepare, offering a fabulous mix of contrasting flavours, textures and colours. The sharp saltiness of the crunchy crostini helps to highlight the delicate taste of the asparagus that follows. Rounded off with a satisfying helping of fresh seafood pasta, this is a beautifully balanced meal.

CROSTINI WITH GARLIC, TOMATO AND ANCHOVY

(see page 41)

ASPARAGUS WITH BALSAMIC VINEGAR AND PARMESAN

(see page 46)

SPAGHETTI WITH PRAWNS

(see page 73)

The day before, make the crostini bases and store in an airtight tin. Prepare individual ingredients for the crostini topping, but do not mix together. Trim the asparagus and shave the Parmesan cheese. Clean and shell the prawns. Place the topping ingredients, asparagus, Parmesan and prawns in covered containers in the fridge. Note that the recipes serve four, so if you are serving just two people, you will need to halve the quantities of ingredients asked for in the recipes.

PM	
12.30	ASSEMBLE the crostini. Preheat the oven for the asparagus.
1.00	SERVE the crostini. Place the asparagus in the oven.
1.20	PUT the water for the pasta on to boil and serve the asparagus.
1.35	COOK the pasta and prepare the sauce (while the pasta is cooking).
1.45	DRAIN the pasta, combine with the sauce and serve.

PREPARATION NOTES

Buy the freshest **PRAWNS** you can find, still in the shell. They should be **RAW** prawns rather than the pre-cooked variety as they will give a superior flavour and texture to the pasta dish. When you have **SHELLED** them, run a sharp knife down the back of the prawns and **WASH** away any gritty black residue that may have collected there.

LUNCH BOX

TIME PLAN

This nourishing lunch is a good match of creamy, rich frittata with two tangy and unusual salads that will retain their freshness even on a hot day. It takes only a few moments to assemble and pack.

COURGETTE FRITTATA
(see page 50)

TOMATO, MINT AND RED ONION SALAD
(see page 153)

ORANGE AND FENNEL SALAD
(see page 157)

PANFORTE
(see page 182)

The panforte can be made up to three weeks in advance and stored in an airtight tin. The night before, prepare and combine all the salad ingredients, but do not add the dressings. Store them in sealed containers in the fridge. Prepare and keep the dressings in separate containers, also refrigerated. Make the frittata and keep, well covered, in the fridge. Note that the recipes used serve four and that quantities of ingredients should be adjusted to suit your own requirements.

In the morning, slice and pack the frittata. Pack the containers of salad and their dressings separately. Wrap and pack slices of panforte.

PM
12.45   POUR the dressings over the salads and mix well to combine.
1.00   SERVE the slices of frittata with the dressed salads. Round off lunch with the panforte.

PREPARATION NOTES

FENNEL is a delicious addition to many dishes and is used WIDELY throughout Italy. Buy only fresh unblemished bulbs. If you try to simply REMOVE and discard any bruised parts, you will find you have very little left, as the layers are very thick and you will lose most of the fennel. To prepare, remove the feathery FRONDS from the top of the fennel with a sharp knife and cut in half. Remove the central core and then SLICE. The fronds can be chopped up and used as a flavouring. Sprinkle any cut fennel with a little LEMON juice, otherwise it will turn brown very quickly.

MID-WEEK LUNCH WITH FAMILY

TIME PLAN

Clear, fresh flavours are the central theme of this quick and easy lunch menu for four. The tangy tomato soup offers a refreshing lead into the subtle seasoning of the chicken and asparagus, while the strawberries in balsamic vinegar make for a rich yet light finish in which the true taste of the fruit really shines through.

CREAMY TOMATO SOUP
(see page 70)

DEVILLED CHICKEN
(see page 122)

ASPARAGUS SALAD
(see page 161)

STRAWBERRIES IN BALSAMIC VINEGAR
(see page 166)

The night before, make the soup and prepare all of the ingredients for the devilled chicken but do not marinate. Trim and blanch the asparagus for the salad and cut up the cherry tomatoes. Make up the salad dressing. Store all the prepared food, except the asparagus, covered, in the fridge. Only chill the asparagus in very hot weather.

PM
12.30 MARINATE the chicken, cover and set aside in a cool place. Combine the salad ingredients in a serving bowl, but do not dress. Leave, covered, in a cool place.

1.00 HEAT the soup and serve. Preheat the grill.

1.15 COOK the chicken under the hot grill until the juices run clear. Dress the salad and serve with the cooked chicken.

1.45 SPRINKLE the balsamic vinegar over the strawberries and serve.

PREPARATION NOTES

The easiest way to prepare ASPARAGUS is to simply bend the ends of the stems with your hand – the asparagus spear will always break at the point where it starts to become TENDER, leaving the woody part behind to be discarded. PEEL the remaining part of the stem with a vegetable peeler until it is the same thickness as the tip. This allows whole asparagus spears (tips and stems) to COOK evenly. Asparagus is a very tender vegetable, so take care not to overcook it.

MID-WEEK LUNCH WITH FRIENDS

MUSHROOM RISOTTO
(see page 98)

SOLE VENETIAN-STYLE
(see page 134)

FRESH TOMATO SALAD WITH COUNTRY BREAD
(see page 151)

BAKED PEACHES STUFFED WITH AMARETTI BISCUITS
(see page 170)

TIME PLAN

All of the dishes, apart from the risotto, can be prepared almost completely in advance, making this a very easy lunch for four. The creamy, flavourful risotto contrasts well with the delicate fish and the juicy salad, and the biscuits blend beautifully with the tang of the peaches.

The night before, slice the mushrooms and make the stock for the risotto (or defrost from the freezer). Halve and stone the peaches and stuff with the amaretti mixture. Cover and store in the fridge.

AM 11.30 CHOP the ingredients for the fresh tomato salad. Combine everything, except the diced bread, in a large serving bowl. Cover and set aside in a cool place. Prepare the ingredients for the sole, again keeping them covered in a cool place.

PM 12.00 DICE and cook the onions for the risotto. Turn off the heat and leave in the pan. Prepare the remaining risotto ingredients and set aside.

12.30 MAKE the risotto according to the recipe.

1.00 ADD the bread to the salad and prepare the dressing. Set both on one side, but do not combine. Serve the risotto.

1.20 COOK the sole and serve. Combine the salad and dressing and serve.

1.45 PREHEAT the oven for the peaches.

2.15 BAKE the stuffed peaches in the hot oven.

2.30 SERVE the peaches, with cream passed around separately.

PREPARATION NOTES

LEMON SOLE is a delicious flat fish that is very thin and will cook through quite quickly. Freshly made WHITE breadcrumbs are essential for coating the FISH when it is cooked Venetian-style. To make them, simply take a loaf of stale white bread and slice up roughly. Remove the crusts, then drop chunks through the feeding tube into a food processor, while the motor is running. Any breadcrumbs not used for coating the sole will keep well in the FREEZER for later use.

WEEKEND LUNCH WITH FAMILY

TIME PLAN

The soup is quite substantial, so just a small amount topped with a dash of extra-virgin olive oil will make an ideal start to this family lunch for four. The chargrilled steak is simpler and quicker to prepare than a full roast, and the lemon ricotta cake provides a zesty ending.

PASTA AND BEAN SOUP

(see page 69)

GRILLED STEAK, FLORENTINE-STYLE, WITH STUFFED MUSHROOMS

(see page 109)

PEAS WITH PANCETTA AND MINT

(see page 146)

LEMON RICOTTA CAKE

(see page 178)

The day or evening before, make the soup. Prepare and stuff the mushrooms and shell the peas. Keep everything, well covered, in the fridge until ready to use. Make the cake and store in a cool place.

PM 12.30 PREHEAT the oven for the mushrooms. Put the water for the peas on to boil. Warm the soup and serve.

1.00 PLACE the stuffed mushrooms in the hot oven. Cook the peas in the boiling water, then drain and keep warm. Brown the pancetta and keep warm.

1.15 COOK the steaks to your preference. Finish off the peas and pancetta and serve with the steak and cooked mushrooms.

1.45 SERVE the cake (warm gently in a low oven for about 10 minutes, if preferred), accompanied by cream and fresh raspberries, if you wish.

PREPARATION NOTES

The lemon RICOTTA cake in this menu is guaranteed to become a firm family FAVOURITE. It is particularly good served warm. One of the best ways to WARM it through is to cut it into serving SLICES first. Then place these in the microwave for about 30 seconds on a MEDIUM heat, just before serving.

WEEKEND LUNCH WITH FRIENDS

This menu for four is designed for maximum impact with minimum effort. The soup is fairly hearty, so do not be tempted to serve too much – make sure you leave your guests room for the dishes that follow. Ice cream is the ideal way to round off such a comforting meal.

THICK VEGETABLE SOUP WITH PESTO

(see page 61)

CHICKEN WITH WHITE WINE, TOMATOES AND VEGETABLES

(see page 121)

POTATO SALAD WITH CAPERS

(see page 158)

LEMON OR COFFEE ICE CREAM

(see page 174 or 177)

Make the ice cream up to two days in advance and store in the freezer. The night before, make the soup and cook the potatoes for the salad. Prepare the other salad ingredients but do not combine with the potatoes. Keep everything, covered, in the fridge.

In the morning, make the chicken casserole and leave to cool on the stove. If it is a very hot day, keep in the fridge until required.

PM

1.00 WARM the soup over a low heat and serve.

1.30 MIX together all the ingredients for the potato salad and set on one side. Heat the chicken casserole until it is piping hot. Transfer to a serving dish, garnish and take to the table. Serve the chicken and let your guests help themselves to the salad.

2.15 TAKE the ice cream out of the freezer and place in the refrigerator to soften for about 20 minutes.

2.35 SERVE the ice cream.

PREPARATION NOTES

When cooking the POTATOES for the salad, you will get the best TEXTURE if they are boiled or steamed whole. The easiest way to check if potatoes are cooked through enough, is to pierce them with a SKEWER – if the potato falls off the end easily they are COOKED; if not, leave them a few minutes more and then test again.

SIMPLE DINNER

TIME PLAN

Almost everything can be prepared well in advance for this easy dinner. The flavours are simple and direct, perfect for a truly relaxing, informal occasion. The chocolate ice-cream slice is very rich, however, so is best balanced with some fresh, juicy berries.

The day before, prepare the beef casserole and the chocolate ice-cream slice. Make the vegetable crudités for the dip, cover with clear film to prevent them drying out and keep refrigerated. If you are serving this menu to two people, remember to halve the quantities of ingredients asked for in the recipes.

PM

7.30 PREPARE the dip and serve warm with the vegetable crudités.

8.00 WARM the beef casserole over a low heat, stirring from time to time. Prepare the mozzarella and tomato salad and serve.

8.30 SERVE the beef, with a helping of "wet" polenta (see page 27), if you wish.

9.00 REMOVE the chocolate ice-cream slice from the freezer and place in the refrigerator for 20 minutes, to soften slightly.

9.20 SERVE the chocolate ice-cream slice with fresh berries.

PREPARATION NOTES

When you are making the ice-cream slice, be CAREFUL not to overwhip the cream. It should be just THICK enough to hold its SHAPE, but not stiff. If it is whipped too much, it will be difficult to FOLD into the mixture and you will end up with LUMPS of frozen cream that will SPOIL the smooth richness of the finished dish.

ROMANTIC DINNER

RISOTTO WITH PRAWNS AND CHAMPAGNE
(see page 101)

VEAL ESCALOPES WITH LEMON AND CAPERS
(see page 117)

OVEN-BAKED POTATOES
(see page 138)

ZABAGLIONE
(see page 165)

TIME PLAN

What could be better for a romantic dinner than a combination of Champagne, succulent, tender veal and warm, melt-in-the-mouth zabaglione? This menu takes a little effort, but the results are truly sensational.

In the morning, collect and measure out all the ingredients (to serve two, halve all the recipe quantities given). Shell the prawns and keep refrigerated. Chop the onion for the risotto and the capers and parsley for the veal. Cover and set aside in a cool place. Separate the eggs for the zabaglione and keep refrigerated, covered with clear film.

PM
6.30 PEEL the potatoes, then chop up and coat in the remaining ingredients.
7.00 PREHEAT the oven for the potatoes.
7.30 PLACE the potatoes in the hot oven. Prepare the risotto (and drink any left-over Champagne!).
7.50 TURN over the potatoes and serve the risotto.
8.15 COOK the veal and serve with the potatoes.
9.00 PREPARE the zabaglione and serve immediately with the sponge-finger biscuits.

PREPARATION NOTES

It is important to use really **THIN** pieces of veal for preparing the escalopes, so that they cook quickly. If you have **TROUBLE** buying veal that is cut in this way, place each piece between two layers of clear film and **BEAT** gently with the end of a rolling pin or a meat mallet until it is thin enough.

MID-WEEK DINNER WITH FAMILY

TIME PLAN

MEATBALLS WITH TOMATO SAUCE AND CRUSTY BREAD

(see page 105)

LIVER WITH ONIONS

(see page 113)

ITALIAN CREAMS

(see page 162)

This is a menu full of strongly flavoured, satisfying family favourites for four. Both the meatballs and bread and the liver with onions, go well with a simple green salad. The Italian creams are traditionally served with fresh berries or a fresh fruit purée, for a mouth-tingling finish.

The night before, make up the meatballs, brown them and leave to cool, then store in the fridge, covered with clear film. Prepare the tomato sauce. Trim and remove any membranes from the liver and cut into thin slices (or ask your butcher to do this for you). Wrap well in clear film and store in the fridge. Make the Italian creams and keep well chilled.

PM
6.30 PREHEAT the oven for the meatballs. Arrange in a baking dish and top with the tomato sauce and cheese. Slice the onions for the liver and, if serving, prepare a green salad, but do not dress.

6.45 PLACE the meatballs in the oven. Sauté the onions for the liver, until they are golden brown. Keep warm on one side.

7.15 REMOVE the meatballs from the oven and serve with crusty bread.

7.45 FINISH cooking the liver and serve. Dress and serve the salad.

8.15 REMOVE the Italian creams from the fridge and serve with berries or a fresh fruit purée, as desired.

PREPARATION NOTES

Good QUALITY liver is now widely available in supermarkets, as well as at the butcher. If possible, buy it ready sliced to the thickness you require, with the MEMBRANES trimmed off. But do check carefully for any remaining membranes before cooking. They can easily be removed by stripping them off with a SHARP knife.

MID-WEEK DINNER WITH FRIENDS

TIME PLAN

Traditional, vibrant, rustic flavours characterize this menu for four. The meaty fish is a good match for the hearty yet fragrant mix of beans, tomatoes and herbs. Use whatever mushrooms are available for the tarts and do not be afraid to experiment with new varieties.

WILD MUSHROOM AND SHALLOT TARTS
(see page 54)

MARINATED SWORDFISH
(see page 130)

WARM CANNELLINI BEANS WITH TOMATOES AND HERBS
(see page 145)

"PICK-ME-UP" TRIFLE
(see page 169)

The day before, make the pastry cases and store in an airtight container. Soak the beans during the day, then cook them in the evening and store in a cool place until ready to use. Prepare the "pick-me-up" trifle and store in the fridge, but leave the dusting of cocoa powder until just before you are ready to serve.

PM

6.00 COOK the mushroom filling for the tarts and set on one side. Prepare the marinade for the swordfish.

7.00 PREHEAT the oven for warming the pastry shells.

7.15 WARM the pastry shells for about 10 minutes. Leave the swordfish to marinate. Prepare the beans, then set aside and keep warm. Reheat the mushroom filling and assemble and serve the tarts.

7.45 COOK the swordfish and serve with the warm beans.

8.15 REMOVE the trifle from the fridge. Dust with the cocoa powder, carry to the table and serve.

PREPARATION NOTES

Making good PASTRY takes a little practice. The important thing to remember is to use a very light touch – the less the pastry is handled, the BETTER. Rub the butter into the flour until it just begins to BLEND in, then stop; do not be tempted to carry on until every little piece disappears. Treat pastry GENTLY and it will always be light and CRISP.

DINNER PARTY

This special menu is so simple to put together, allowing the cook plenty of time with guests. The creaminess of the gnocchi and gratin is beautifully balanced by the pungent aromas of the fresh herbs and tomatoes. A truly heavenly dessert rounds off the evening perfectly.

SEMOLINA GNOCCHI WITH FRESH TOMATO SAUCE
(see page 93)

LEG OF LAMB WITH HERB CRUST
(see page 114)

POTATO AND HERB GRATIN
(see page 142)

ICE CREAM WITH ESPRESSO AND FRANGELICO
(see page 173)

The night before, prepare the gnocchi dish and the lamb. Keep them, covered, in the fridge. Scoop ice cream into individual dishes and place in the freezer. Remember that the recipes are written to serve just four people, so you may need to increase the quantities of ingredients. If you are serving eight, for example, simply double them.

PM

6.30 PREHEAT the oven.

7.00 PLACE the prepared lamb in the hot oven.

7.40 ADD the prepared gnocchi dish to the oven, alongside the lamb. Prepare the potato gratin.

8.00 REMOVE the gnocchi from the oven and serve. Put the potato gratin into the oven.

8.15 CHECK the lamb and if cooked, remove from the oven and leave in a warm place to rest for 15 minutes.

8.30 SERVE the lamb with the potato gratin.

9.15 REMOVE the ice cream from the freezer, top with the espresso and Frangelico liqueur and serve immediately.

PREPARATION NOTES

When you buy the leg of LAMB, make sure that you ask the butcher to cut PARTIALLY through the base of the BONE. This will make the joint much easier to carve. Remember, too, that the meat will also slice up more easily if it is allowed to stand, in a WARM place, for 10–15 minutes after it has finished cooking.

DRINKS PARTY

TIME PLAN

A drinks party is a great way to entertain a large number of people with ease. As well as finger-food that can be passed around, try to include several buffet dishes, for eating with a fork, to which guests can help themselves.

CROSTINI WITH GORGONZOLA AND BLACK OLIVE TAPENADE
(see page 42)

DEEP-FRIED RICE BALLS
(see page 57)

CHARGRILLED VEGETABLE SALAD
(see page 34)

AUBERGINE WITH TOMATO SAUCE AND CHEESE
(see page 38)

BAKED MUSSELS WITH CRISPY HERB BREADCRUMBS
(see page 37)

The day before, make the crostini and store in an airtight container. Prepare the tapenade and store in the fridge. Prepare the rice balls for deep-frying and place, covered, in the fridge. Make the sauce to accompany them and make up the aubergine, tomato and cheese dish, ready to go into the oven. Store both in the fridge, covered. Chargrill all the salad vegetables and prepare the dressing, then store separately in a cool place. Clean the mussels thoroughly and keep, covered, in the fridge. Note that this menu will serve eight to ten people, so you will need to adjust the quantities of ingredients for larger numbers.

PM

6.30 PREHEAT the oven for the aubergine dish.

7.00 PLACE the aubergine dish in the hot oven. Prepare the filling for the mussels. Cook the mussels, discarding any that do not open.

7.20 REMOVE the baked aubergine dish from the oven and leave to cool slightly. Spread the topping on the crostini. Assemble and dress the salad. Prepare the stuffed mussels. Heat the oil for the rice balls.

7.30 COOK the rice balls until golden and drain. Place the tomato sauce to accompany them in a bowl. Arrange all the food on platters and serve.

PREPARATION NOTES

It is very important to make sure that the MUSSELS you use are very fresh. Empty them into a large sink of cold water and CLEAN them well, removing any barnacles and the "beard" with a sharp knife. Discard any mussels that remain OPEN at this point, as this indicates that the mussel is not fresh.

INDEX